The Ultimate Mediterranean Air Fryer Cookbook

1500 Days of Effortless and Flavorful Air Fryer Recipes with a 28-Day Meal Plan to Savor the Mediterranean Cuisine | Full Color Edition

Tracy G. Woolard

CW00457140

Copyright© 2023 By Tracy G. Woolard Rights Reserved

This book is copyright protected. It is only for personal use. You cannot amend, distribute, sell, use, quote or paraphrase any part of the content within this book, without the consent of the author or publisher.

Under no circumstances will any blame or legal responsibility be held against the publisher, or author, for any damages, reparation, or monetary loss due to the information contained within this book, either directly or indirectly.

Disclaimer Notice:

Please note the information contained within this document is for educational and entertainment purposes only. All effort has been executed to present accurate, up to date, reliable, complete information. No warranties of any kind are declared or implied. Readers acknowledge that the author is not engaged in the rendering of legal, financial, medical or professional advice. The content within this book has been derived from various sources. Please consult a licensed professional before attempting any techniques outlined in this book.

By reading this document, the reader agrees that under no circumstances is the author responsible for any losses, direct or indirect, that are incurred as a result of the use of the information contained within this document, including, but not limited to, errors, omissions, or inaccuracies.

Editor: LYN
Cover Art: ABR
Interior Design: FAIZAN
Food stylist: JO

Table Of Contents

Introduction

Welcome to the culinary journey. In the pages that follow, you are about to embark on a gastronomic adventure that fuses the health-conscious benefits of air frying with the rich and diverse flavors of Mediterranean cuisine. This cookbook stands as a testament to the harmonious marriage of modern technology and timeless culinary traditions.

The Mediterranean diet has long captured the imagination of food enthusiasts worldwide. Renowned for its emphasis on fresh ingredients, wholesome grains, heart-healthy fats, and vibrant colors, this culinary tradition is a celebration of both flavor and nutrition. It's a way of eating that nourishes the body and soul, while also promoting overall well-being. In recent years, the advent of the air fryer has breathed new life into this cherished culinary heritage, allowing for the creation of dishes that are both delicious and health-conscious.

In the pages of this cookbook, you will find a collection of recipes that pay homage to the Mediterranean way of life. From the sun-soaked coasts of Greece to the aromatic kitchens of Italy, each recipe has been carefully curated to capture the essence of this region's diverse cuisines. and what's more, these dishes have been adapted to make the most of the air fryer's innovative technology, allowing you to enjoy the flavors you love with a lighter touch.

Whether you're a seasoned cook or a kitchen novice, you'll find something to inspire you within these pages. From crispy falafel bites to succulent olive and feta-stuffed chicken breasts, each recipe has been crafted to deliver on taste, texture, and simplicity. The air fryer's ability to achieve the perfect balance between crispiness and tenderness will leave you wondering why you haven't been cooking this way all along.

Beyond the recipes themselves, the Mediterranean Air Fryer cookbook also serves as a guide to understanding the principles of air frying. You'll learn about the science behind this cooking method, why it's considered a healthier alternative to traditional frying, and tips to ensure your dishes turn out picture-perfect every time. Whether you're looking to cut down on oil intake or simply explore new culinary horizons, the air fryer is a tool that will undoubtedly revolutionize the way you approach cooking.

As you turn the pages and discover the joys of Mediterranean-inspired dishes brought to life through the air fryer, remember that this cookbook is more than just a compilation of recipes. It's a tribute to the art of cooking, the appreciation of diverse flavors, and the pursuit of a balanced and fulfilling lifestyle. So, let your taste buds wander through these pages, and may the "Mediterranean Air Fryer Cookbook" become an indispensable companion on your culinary voyage.

Here's to the delight of savoring sumptuous meals that honor tradition while embracing innovation—a feast for the senses and a nourishment for the soul.

Buon appetito and enjoy the journey!

Chapter 1

Mediterranean Air Fryer Delights

Unveiling the Mediterranean Diet

In a world brimming with diets and nutritional trends, the Mediterranean Diet stands as a timeless beacon of both wellness and indulgence. Rooted in the cultural traditions of the Mediterranean region, this diet is not merely a regimen but a harmonious way of life that has captured the attention and admiration of health-conscious individuals and food enthusiasts alike. Combining a wealth of fresh ingredients, culinary mastery, and a philosophy of balanced living, the Mediterranean Diet represents a culinary tapestry that is as diverse as it is nourishing.

At its core, the Mediterranean Diet emphasizes the consumption of whole, unprocessed foods that have been staples in the diets of countries like Greece, Italy, Spain, and southern France. Fruits, vegetables, legumes, nuts, seeds, whole grains, and olive oil form the foundation of this diet, delivering an abundance of essential nutrients, fiber, and healthy fats. These elements work in tandem to nurture overall health and well-being.

One of the distinguishing features of the Mediterranean Diet is its focus on olive oil, a prized source of monounsaturated fats. These fats, in particular, have been associated with reduced risk factors for cardiovascular diseases. The Mediterranean region's reliance on olive oil as a primary fat source rather than saturated fats found in animal products has contributed to the diet's reputation for supporting heart health.

In addition to the prominence of plant-based foods, the Mediterranean Diet also embraces lean sources of protein, such as fish and poultry, while moderating the consumption of red meat. Seafood, a staple in Mediterranean coastal communities, offers not only a lean source of protein but also a rich supply of omega-3 fatty acids, which have been linked to improved cognitive function and reduced inflammation.

Wine, particularly red wine, is often enjoyed in moderation within the Mediterranean Diet. This practice is not only symbolic of conviviality but also a source of resveratrol, an antioxidant believed to contribute to heart health. However, it's important to note that moderation is key, and the diet discourages excessive alcohol consumption.

Equally significant is the Mediterranean lifestyle's encouragement of communal dining and slow, mindful eating. Meals are regarded as opportunities for connection and relaxation, fostering a healthy relationship with food and promoting better digestion. The Mediterranean Diet embodies the idea that nourishment goes beyond physical sustenance; it's about savoring the experience of sharing a meal and embracing the sensory delight of flavors, textures, and aromas.

Research has consistently shown that the Mediterranean Diet offers a spectrum of health benefits. From reducing the risk of chronic diseases like diabetes and hypertension to promoting weight management and longevity, its holistic approach to nutrition transcends fads and fleeting trends. As an eating pattern that has evolved over centuries, it defies the transient nature of diets by promoting sustainable and enjoyable eating practices.

In today's fast-paced world, the Mediterranean Diet serves as a reminder of the significance of time-honored traditions and their power to nourish the body and soul. It speaks to the idea that food is not merely sustenance but an expression of culture, heritage, and well-being. By embracing the vibrant colors, fragrant herbs, and wholesome ingredients of the Mediterranean Diet, individuals are not just adopting a way of eating; they are embracing a philosophy that reverberates through every bite and resonates in every aspect of life.

Ingredients at the Heart of Mediterranean Cooking

Mediterranean cuisine is a testament to the harmonious marriage of simplicity and complexity, and at the core of this culinary tradition lie a handful of ingredients that have stood the test of time. Rooted in the bounties of the land and the sea, Mediterranean cooking celebrates the vibrant colors, rich aromas, and robust flavors that these ingredients bring to the table. From sun-kissed vegetables to luscious olives, the Mediterranean pantry reflects a tapestry of cultures, histories, and nutritional wisdom.

OLIVE OIL: THE LIQUID GOLD

At the pinnacle of the Mediterranean pantry reigns olive oil—a true elixir of both culinary and health virtues. Celebrated for its distinctive flavor, olive oil also boasts an abundance of monounsaturated fats, which are linked to reducing the risk of heart disease. This versatile ingredient graces salads, sautés, and dips, infusing each dish with its golden hue and lush aroma.

TOMATOES: THE VERSATILE ALL-STAR

Tomatoes, with their radiant red hue, bring a burst of sunshine to Mediterranean dishes. From vibrant sauces to refreshing salads, tomatoes offer a delectable balance of sweetness and acidity. They are also rich in lycopene, an antioxidant associated with various health benefits, including promoting skin health and reducing the risk of certain cancers.

FRESH HERBS: THE FRAGRANT ELIXIR

No Mediterranean dish is complete without the presence of fragrant herbs. Basil, rosemary, oregano, thyme, and parsley are just a few of the aromatic treasures that infuse dishes with depth and character. These herbs not only add flavors that evoke the Mediterranean landscape but also contribute essential nutrients and compounds that promote well-being.

FISH AND SEAFOOD: THE OCEAN'S BOUNTY

Given the Mediterranean's proximity to the sea, fish and seafood hold a revered place in the cuisine. Rich in omega-3 fatty acids and lean protein, seafood varieties like salmon, sardines, and anchovies not only tantalize taste buds but also support heart health and brain function. Grilled, baked, or stewed, fish and seafood showcase the simplicity and brilliance of Mediterranean cooking.

LEGUMES: THE HEARTY PROTEIN SOURCE

Lentils, chickpeas, and beans serve as the humble yet hearty backbone of Mediterranean meals. These legumes provide plant-based protein, fiber, and an array of vitamins and minerals. Whether simmered into soups, blended into dips, or incorporated into salads, legumes showcase the diet's commitment to wholesome nutrition and sustainable eating.

CHEESES: THE DAIRY DELIGHTS

From crumbly feta to velvety ricotta, Mediterranean cheeses lend a touch of indulgence to the diet. While consumed in moderation, these cheeses provide a source of calcium and protein. Their diverse textures and flavors complement various dishes, from savory pastries to refreshing salads.

FRUITS: THE SWEET SPLENDOR

Fresh fruits are emblematic of the Mediterranean lifestyle's affinity for seasonal and colorful produce. Figs, pomegranates, citrus fruits, and grapes make appearances in both sweet and savory preparations, adding a touch of natural sweetness and a burst of vitamins and antioxidants.

WHOLE GRAINS: THE NUTRIENT-RICH STAPLES

Whole grains like barley, bulgur, and farro form the basis of many Mediterranean dishes. Their complex carbohydrates provide sustained energy and dietary fiber, contributing to digestive health and satiety. These grains are often incorporated into salads, stews, and side dishes, adding texture and depth to every bite.

The Mediterranean pantry is a treasure trove of ingredients that not only tantalize the taste buds but also offer a wealth of health benefits. The symphony of flavors, colors, and textures that emerges from these components creates a culinary experience that nourishes both the body and the soul. At the heart of Mediterranean cooking lies a profound respect for the interconnectedness of nature, culture, and gastronomy—an ethos that continues to inspire and captivate those who embark on this culinary journey.

The Art and Science of Air Frying

In the realm of modern culinary innovation, the emergence of the air fryer has revolutionized the way we cook and savor our favorite dishes. Beyond its sleek design and user-friendly interface lies a marriage of artistry and scientific principles that reimagines traditional cooking methods. The art and science of air frying converge to offer a culinary experience that's both flavorful and health-conscious.

THE ART OF TEXTURE AND FLAVOR

Air frying is an art that promises a delicate balance of texture—crispy on the outside, tender on the inside—without the need for excessive oil. The technique involves circulating superheated air around the food, resulting in a Maillard reaction—a process that creates a golden-brown crust while retaining the food's natural moisture. From perfectly crisp fries to succulent chicken, air frying preserves the mouthwatering qualities of fried foods while significantly reducing the amount of oil used.

This artistry extends to the creation of complex flavors. The air fryer's efficient heating mechanism allows for quicker caramelization, intensifying the taste of ingredients and infusing them with a delectable depth. Spices, herbs, and marinades meld harmoniously with the air frying process, enhancing the final dish's overall appeal.

THE SCIENCE BEHIND THE SIZZLE

Behind every crisp and flavorful bite in the air-fried realm lies a fascinating science that transforms the cooking process. Unlike traditional frying methods that submerge food in oil, air frying relies on the Maillard reaction and convection currents to create the desired outcome.

The Maillard reaction, triggered by the combination of amino acids and reducing sugars in food, produces those irresistible aromas and flavors we associate with well-cooked meals. Air fryers facilitate this reaction at a faster rate due to their ability to maintain a consistent and high temperature. The result is a crispy exterior that envelops succulent interiors.

Convection currents within the air fryer play a crucial role in distributing heat evenly. A fan circulates the superheated air around the food, ensuring uniform cooking and eliminating the need for constant flipping or turning. This scientific precision contributes to achieving consistent results with minimal effort.

HEALTH-CONSCIOUS COOKING

The science of air frying extends to its health-conscious benefits as well. By using significantly less oil than traditional frying methods, air frying reduces the caloric content of dishes without compromising on taste. The minimized oil absorption also means that dishes are lighter on the digestive system.

Additionally, air frying decreases the formation of harmful compounds that can arise from deep-frying at high temperatures. The Maillard reaction occurring in the air fryer produces fewer acrylamides—a group of chemicals associated with the browning process—compared to traditional frying. This aligns with the broader trend towards healthier cooking practices.

In the symphony of culinary transformation, air frying harmonizes artistry and science to bring about a delightful shift in the culinary landscape. From crispy delights to savory sensations, the air fryer showcases the fusion of innovation and tradition, granting us the joy of savoring our favorite dishes with a lighter touch and a deeper appreciation for the culinary craft.

Discovering the Mediterranean Diet Meets Air Frying

The intersection of the Mediterranean diet and air frying unveils a culinary synergy that marries ancient traditions with modern innovation, resulting in a harmonious blend of health-conscious cooking and vibrant flavors. The Mediterranean diet, renowned for its emphasis on wholesome ingredients and heart-healthy fats, seamlessly integrates with the air fryer's ability to create crispy, delectable dishes with minimal oil.

NOURISHING TRADITION WITH TECHNOLOGY

The Mediterranean diet, rooted in the culinary practices of Mediterranean coastal regions, champions an abundance of fresh fruits, vegetables, whole grains, lean proteins, and olive oil—a hallmark of the region's renowned longevity and well-being. This dietary philosophy aligns harmoniously with the air fryer's approach to cooking, where the reduction of oil usage resonates with the diet's commitment to healthy fats.

CRISPNESS MEETS NUTRITIONAL VALUE

Air frying, with its innovative circulation of superheated air, achieves a splendid crispness that mimics the indulgence of deep-fried fare. However, it does so with far less oil, enhancing the nutritional profile of dishes without compromising on taste. The union of Mediterranean staples and air frying's precision creates dishes that are as delightful to the palate as they are beneficial to the body.

PRESERVING FLAVORS, ENHANCING BENEFITS

When Mediterranean ingredients like olive oil, fresh herbs, and lean proteins meet the air fryer, their flavors are intensified and elevated. The air fryer's technology facilitates the Maillard reaction, creating a golden crust that locks in the rich, authentic flavors inherent to Mediterranean cuisine. This fusion ensures that dishes not only satisfy the taste buds but also align with the diet's principles of balance and vitality.

EMPOWERING WELLNESS THROUGH CULINARY EXPLORATION

The fusion of the Mediterranean diet and air frying encourages a culinary adventure that empowers wellness without sacrificing enjoyment. It offers a gateway to exploring beloved Mediterranean classics—from crispy falafel to succulent grilled fish—in a way that embraces both tradition and innovation.

EMBRACING A DELICIOUS FUTURE

Discovering the harmony between the Mediterranean diet and air frying opens a door to a world of culinary possibilities. It embodies the essence of progress without forsaking heritage—a journey that prioritizes both nourishment and indulgence. As we embark on this delightful exploration, we embrace a future where wellness and flavor converge to create a vibrant and fulfilling way of eating.

Chapter 2

28-Day Meal Plan

Week 1: Embracing the Mediterranean Diet

Congratulations on taking the first step towards a healthier lifestyle with the Mediterranean Diet! This week marks the beginning of a transformative journey that will reward you with improved well-being and vitality. Embrace the simplicity and richness of this diet, focusing on nourishing your body with wholesome, nutrient-packed foods. As you make mindful choices, remember that every small change you make is a step closer to a healthier you. Stay committed and motivated, and soon you'll begin to experience the positive impact of this new way of eating.

Meal Plan	Breakfast	Lunch	Dinner	Snack
Day-1	Ground Pork Casserole	Bacon Wrapped Herb Chicken	Oregano Fish Fingers	Sea Salt Beet Chips
Day-2	Ground Pork Casserole	Bacon Wrapped Herb Chicken	Oregano Fish Fingers	Sea Salt Beet Chips
Day-3	Ground Pork Casserole	Bacon Wrapped Herb Chicken	Oregano Fish Fingers	Sea Salt Beet Chips
Day-4	Ground Pork Casserole	Bacon Wrapped Herb Chicken	Grilled Salmon Fillets	Sea Salt Beet Chips
Day-5	Ground Pork Casserole	Bacon Wrapped Herb Chicken	Grilled Salmon Fillets	Sea Salt Beet Chips

Shopping List for Week 1

PROTEINS:

- 2 cups ground pork
- 1 chicken breast
- 6 slices of bacon
- 1-pound tilapia fillet
- 2 salmon fillets
- 2 eggs, beaten

VEGETABLES:

- 2 jalapeno peppers
- 4 medium beets
- Hummus (for serving)

MISCELLANEOUS:

- 1 teaspoon coconut oil
- 1 teaspoon chili flakes
- ½ teaspoon ground turmeric
- ½ teaspoon basil, dried
- ½ teaspoon parsley, dried
- ½ teaspoon paprika
- Salt and pepper
- 1 tablespoon soft cheese
- 1 teaspoon dried oregano
- 1 teaspoon avocado oil
- 4 tablespoons olive oil
- 1 teaspoon liquid stevia
- 1/3 cup of light soy sauce
- 1/3 cup of water
- Salt and black pepper to taste

Week 2: Diving Deeper into Mediterranean Delights

As you enter Week 2, you're delving deeper into the Mediterranean way of life. Embrace the joy of discovering new flavors and aromas that will awaken your taste buds and inspire your culinary adventures. Your commitment to choosing fresh, natural ingredients is already paying off, and you'll soon notice positive changes in your energy levels and overall well-being. Stay focused on the journey, and remember that each day brings you closer to unlocking the full potential of this nourishing diet.

Meal Plan	Breakfast	Lunch	Dinner	Snack
Day-1	Greek Bread	Italian-Style Pork Center Cut	Italian Herb Potatoes	Greece Style Cake
Day-2	Greek Bread	Italian-Style Pork Center Cut	Italian Herb Potatoes	Greece Style Cake
Day-3	Greek Bread	Italian-Style Pork Center Cut	Italian Herb Potatoes	Greece Style Cake
Day-4	Greek Bread	Italian-Style Pork Center Cut	Grilled Salmon Fillets	Greece Style Cake
Day-5	Greek Bread	Italian-Style Pork Center Cut	Grilled Salmon Fillets	Greece Style Cake

Shopping List for Week 2

PROTEINS:
- 2 pounds pork center cut
- 2 salmon fillets
- 7 eggs

VEGETABLES:
- 1 pound potatoes

MISCELLANEOUS:
- 2 tablespoons Greek yogurt
- ½ teaspoon baking powder
- ½ cup almond flour
- 1 teaspoon butter, melted
- 2 tablespoons olive oil
- 1 tablespoon Italian herb mix
- 1 teaspoon red pepper flakes

- Sea salt and freshly ground black pepper
- 4 tablespoons olive oil
- 1 teaspoon granulated garlic
- 1 teaspoon cayenne pepper
- Salt and black pepper to taste
- 1 teaspoon liquid stevia
- 1/3 cup of light soy sauce
- 1/3 cup of water
- Salt and black pepper to taste
- 1 teaspoon vanilla extract
- 1 teaspoon baking powder
- 4 tablespoons Erythritol
- 1 cup Plain yogurt

Week 3: Unleashing the Mediterranean Secrets

Week 3 brings a sense of empowerment as you uncover the secrets of the Mediterranean Diet's numerous health benefits. By now, you've experienced firsthand how this way of eating can transform your body and mind. As you continue to fuel your body with wholesome foods, embrace the sense of clarity and vitality that comes with it. Celebrate your progress and remember that you have the strength and determination to carry this newfound lifestyle beyond the four weeks. Let the Mediterranean Diet become a part of who you are and bring out the best version of yourself.

Meal Plan	Breakfast	Lunch	Dinner	Snack
Day-1	Lemon Bread	Parsley Lemon Turkey	Trout with Mint	Cream Cheese Pie
Day-2	Lemon Bread	Parsley Lemon Turkey	Trout with Mint	Cream Cheese Pie
Day-3	Lemon Bread	Parsley Lemon Turkey	Trout with Mint	Cream Cheese Pie
Day-4	Lemon Bread	Parsley Lemon Turkey	Lentil Stuffed Eggplant	Cream Cheese Pie
Day-5	Lemon Bread	Parsley Lemon Turkey	Lentil Stuffed Eggplant	Cream Cheese Pie

Shopping List for Week 3

PROTEINS:
- 2 pounds turkey wings
- 4 rainbow trout
- 3 eggs

VEGETABLES:
- 1 medium eggplant
- 1 onion
- 2 garlic cloves
- 1 cup parsley
- Lemon (for zest and juice)

MISCELLANEOUS:
- 3 cups all-purpose flour
- 3 tablespoons poppy seeds

- 2 cups sugar
- 1½ cups milk
- 1½ teaspoon baking powder
- 1 teaspoon salt
- 1 cup vegetable oil
- 2 teaspoons fresh lemon juice
- 1 teaspoon pure vanilla extract
- 2 tablespoons lemon zest
- 2 tablespoons olive oil
- 1/2 teaspoon garlic powder
- 1/2 teaspoon onion powder
- 1 teaspoon poultry seasoning mix
- 2 tablespoons fresh parsley
- 3 garlic cloves (for trout recipe)
- ½ cup mint (for trout recipe)
- 3 tablespoons Erythritol
- 1 tablespoon coconut oil

Week 4: Celebrating Your Transformative Journey

Congratulations! You've made it to Week 4, and you're now fully immersed in the Mediterranean lifestyle. Your commitment to wholesome, unprocessed foods has yielded tremendous rewards, both physically and mentally. Embrace this final week with gratitude and a sense of accomplishment. Continue enjoying a rainbow of fresh produce, indulge in occasional glasses of red wine, and prioritize regular physical activity. By now, you'll likely notice improved digestion, glowing skin, and a balanced weight. As you conclude this transformative journey, remember that the Mediterranean Diet isn't just a month-long endeavor; it's a lifelong celebration of health and well-being. Embrace this lifestyle with joy, and may it bring you lasting vitality and happiness.

Meal Plan	Breakfast	Lunch	Dinner	Snack
Day-1	Whole Wheat Blueberry Muffins	Italian Pulled Pork Ragu	Mediterranean-Pita Wraps	Ricotta Cookies
Day-2	Whole Wheat Blueberry Muffins	Italian Pulled Pork Ragu	Mediterranean-Pita Wraps	Ricotta Cookies
Day-3	Whole Wheat Blueberry Muffins	Italian Pulled Pork Ragu	Mediterranean-Pita Wraps	Ricotta Cookies
Day-4	Whole Wheat Blueberry Muffins	Italian Pulled Pork Ragu	Mediterranean Veggie Mix	Ricotta Cookies
Day-5	Whole Wheat Blueberry Muffins	Italian Pulled Pork Ragu	Mediterranean Veggie Mix	Ricotta Cookies

Shopping List for Week 4

PROTEINS:

- 2 pounds beef shoulder
- 1 pound mackerel fish fillets
- 2 large egg

VEGETABLES:

- ½ cup blueberries
- 2 garlic cloves
- 1 large zucchini
- 1 green pepper
- 1 large parsnip
- 4 cherry tomatoes
- 1 medium carrot

MISCELLANEOUS:

- Olive oil cooking spray
- ½ cup unsweetened applesauce
- ¼ cup raw honey
- ½ cup nonfat plain Greek yogurt
- 1 teaspoon vanilla extract
- ½ teaspoon baking powder
- ½ teaspoon salt
- 1 cup ricotta cheese
- 1 cup coconut flour
- 2 tablespoons swerve

Chapter 3

Breakfast

Honey-Apricot Granola with Greek Yogurt

Prep time: 10 minutes | Cook time: 30 minutes | Serves 6

- 1 cup rolled oats
- ¼ cup dried apricots, diced
- ¼ cup almond slivers
- ¼ cup walnuts, chopped
- ¼ cup pumpkin seeds
- ¼ cup hemp hearts
- ¼ to ⅓ cup raw honey, plus more for drizzling
- 1 tablespoon olive oil
- 1 teaspoon ground cinnamon
- ¼ teaspoon ground nutmeg
- ¼ teaspoon salt
- 2 tablespoons sugar-free dark chocolate chips (optional)
- 3 cups nonfat plain Greek yogurt

1. Preheat the air fryer to 260°F. Line the air fryer basket with parchment paper.
2. In a large bowl, combine the oats, apricots, almonds, walnuts, pumpkin seeds, hemp hearts, honey, olive oil, cinnamon, nutmeg, and salt, mixing so that the honey, oil, and spices are well distributed.
3. Pour the mixture onto the parchment paper and spread it into an even layer.
4. Bake for 10 minutes, then shake or stir and spread back out into an even layer. Continue baking for 10 minutes more, then repeat the process of shaking or stirring the mixture. Bake for an additional 10 minutes before removing from the air fryer.
5. Allow the granola to cool completely before stirring in the chocolate chips (if using) and pouring into an airtight container for storage.
6. For each serving, top ½ cup Greek yogurt with ⅓ cup granola and a drizzle of honey, if needed.

PER SERVING

Calories: 342 | Total Fat: 16g | Saturated Fat: 4g | Protein: 20g | Total Carbohydrates: 31g | Fiber: 4g | Sugar: 19g | Cholesterol: 6mg

Avocado Bake

Prep time: 10 minutes | Cook time: 20 minutes |Serves 2

- 1 avocado, pitted, halved
- 2 eggs
- 1 oz Parmesan, grated
- ½ teaspoon ground nutmeg

1. Crack the eggs in the avocado hole and top them with Parmesan and ground nutmeg.
2. Then put the eggplants in the air fryer basket and cook at 375F for 20 minutes.

PER SERVING

Calories: 316 | Fat: 27.2 | Fiber: 6.8 | Carbs: 9.8 | Protein: 12

Ground Pork Casserole

Prep time: 15 minutes | Cook time: 25 minutes |Serves 6

- 2 jalapeno peppers, sliced
- 2 cups ground pork
- 1 cup Cheddar cheese, shredded
- 1 teaspoon coconut oil
- 1 teaspoon chili flakes
- ½ teaspoon ground turmeric

1. Grease the air fryer basket with coconut oil.
2. Then mix ground pork with jalapeno peppers, chili flakes, and ground turmeric.
3. Put the mixture in the air fryer basket and flatten it. Top the mixture with Cheddar cheese.
4. Cook the casserole at 380F for 25 minutes.

PER SERVING

Calories: 395 | Fat: 28.8 | Fiber: 0.2 | Carbs: 0.7 | Protein: 31.6

Spinach & Parsley Baked Omelet

Prep time: 5 minutes | Cook time: 10 minutes | Serves 1

- 1 teaspoon olive oil
- 3 eggs
- 3 tablespoons ricotta cheese
- 1 tablespoon parsley, chopped
- ¼ cup spinach, chopped
- Salt and pepper to taste

1. Preheat your air fryer to 330°Fahrenheit.
2. Whisk eggs adding salt and pepper as seasoning.
3. Heat the olive oil in air fryer.
4. Stir in the ricotta, spinach, and parsley with eggs.
5. Pour the egg mixture into baking dish and cook in air fryer for 10-minutes. Serve warm.

PER SERVING

Calories: 235 | Total Fat: 9.2g | Carbs: 8.4g | Protein: 11.6g

English Breakfast

Prep time: 5 minutes | Cook time: 20 minutes | Serves 4

- 8 medium sausages
- 8 slices of back bacon
- 4 eggs
- 8 slices of toast
- 1 can baked beans
- 2 tomatoes, sliced, sautė
- ½ cup mushrooms, finely sliced, sautė
- 1 tablespoon olive oil

1. Preheat your air fryer to 320°Fahrenheit.
2. Heat olive oil in saucepan over medium-high heat.
3. Add mushrooms to pan and sautė for a few minutes.
4. Remove mushrooms from pan and set aside, add tomatoes to pan and sautė for a few minutes then set aside.
5. Place your sausages and bacon into your air fryer and cook for 10-minutes.
6. Place the baked beans into a ramekin and your (cracked) eggs in another ramekin and cook for an additional 10-minutes at 390°Fahrenheit. Serve warm.

PER SERVING

Calories: 243 | Total Fat: 12.3g | Carbs: 10.5g | Protein: 16.3g

Whole Wheat Blueberry Muffins

Prep time: 10 minutes | Cook time: 15 minutes | Serves 6

- Olive oil cooking spray
- ½ cup unsweetened applesauce
- ¼ cup raw honey
- ½ cup nonfat plain Greek yogurt
- 1 teaspoon vanilla extract
- 1 large egg
- 1½ cups plus 1 tablespoon whole wheat flour, divided
- ½ teaspoon baking soda
- ½ teaspoon baking powder
- ½ teaspoon salt
- ½ cup blueberries, fresh or frozen

1. Preheat the air fryer to 360°F. Lightly coat the inside of six silicone muffin cups or a six-cup muffin tin with olive oil cooking spray.
2. In a large bowl, combine the applesauce, honey, yogurt, vanilla, and egg and mix until smooth.
3. Sift in 1½ cups of the flour, the baking soda, baking powder, and salt into the wet mixture, then stir until just combined.
4. In a small bowl, toss the blueberries with the remaining 1 tablespoon flour, then fold the mixture into the muffin batter.
5. Divide the mixture evenly among the prepared muffin cups and place into the basket of the air fryer. Bake for 12 to 15 minutes, or until golden brown on top and a toothpick inserted into the middle of one of the muffins comes out clean.
6. Allow to cool for 5 minutes before serving.

PER SERVING

Calories: 186 | Total Fat: 2g | Saturated Fat: 0g | Protein: 7g | Total Carbohydrates: 38g |

Fiber: 4g | Sugar: 16g | Cholesterol: 32mg

Avocado Spread

Prep time: 10 minutes | Cook time: 10 minutes |Serves 4

- 1 teaspoon garlic powder
- 1 avocado, pitted, peeled, chopped
- 1 tablespoon pork rinds, chopped
- 1 egg
- 1 tablespoon cream cheese

1. Preheat the air fryer to 375F.
2. Mix beaten egg with pork rinds and pour the mixture in the air fryer.
3. Cook it at 385F for 10 minutes. Stir the cooked egg mixture well.
4. Then mix it with garlic powder, avocado, and cream cheese. Blend the mixture well.

PER SERVING

Calories: 149 | Fat: 13 | Fiber: 3.4 | Carbs: 5 | Protein: 4.9

Morning Veggies On Toast

Prep time: 6 minutes | Cook time: 11 minutes | Serves 4

- 1 tablespoon olive oil
- ½ cup soft goat cheese
- 2 tablespoons softened butter
- 4 slices French bread
- 2 green onions, sliced
- 1 small yellow squash, sliced
- 1 cup button mushrooms, sliced
- 1 red bell pepper, cut into strips

1. Sprinkle your air fryer with olive oil and preheat it to 350°Fahrenheit.
2. Mix the red bell peppers, squash, mushrooms and green onions, cook them for 7-minutes.
3. Place vegetables on a plate and set aside.
4. Spread the bread slices with butter and place into air fryer, with butter side up.
5. Toast for 4-minutes.
6. Spread the goat cheese on toasted bread and top with veggies. Serve warm.

PER SERVING

Calories: 243 | Total Fat: 10.3g | Carbs: 8.5g | Protein: 9.3g

Kielbasa Scramble

Prep time: 10 minutes | Cook time: 8 minutes |Serves 4

- 8 eggs, beaten
- 1 teaspoon dried parsley
- 3 oz kielbasa, chopped
- 1 teaspoon coconut oil
- 1 teaspoon dried oregano

1. Preheat the air fryer to 385F.
2. Then toss coconut oil in the air fryer basket and melt it.
3. Add kielbasa and cook it for 2 minutes

per side.
4. After this, add eggs, parsley, and oregano.
5. Stir the mixture well and cook it for 4 minutes. Stir the meal again.

PER SERVING

Calories: 185 | Fat: 13.7 | Fiber: 0.2 | Carbs: 1.8 | Protein: 13.9

Baked Eggs & Sausage Muffins

Prep time: 5 minutes | Cook time: 20 minutes | Serves 2

- 3 eggs
- ¼ cup cream
- 2 sausages, boiled
- Chopped fresh herbs
- Sea salt to taste
- 4 tablespoons cheese, grated
- 1 piece of bread, sliced lengthwise

1. Preheat your air fryer to 360°Fahrenheit.
2. Break the eggs in a bowl, add cream, and scramble.
3. Grease 3 muffin cups with cooking spray.
4. Add equal amounts of egg mixture into each.
5. Arrange sliced sausages and bread slices into muffin cups, sinking into egg mixture.
6. Sprinkle the tops with cheese, and salt to taste.
7. Cook the muffins for 20-minutes.
8. Season with fresh herbs and serve warm.

PER SERVING

Calories: 242 | Total Fat: 12.5g | Carbs: 10.2g | Protein: 14.3g

Morning Time Sausages

Prep time: 10 minutes | Cook time: 12 minutes | Serves 6

- 7-ounces ground chicken
- 7-ounces ground pork
- 1 teaspoon ground coriander
- 1 teaspoon basil, dried
- ½ teaspoon nutmeg
- 1 teaspoon olive oil
- 1 teaspoon minced garlic
- 1 tablespoon coconut flour
- 1 egg
- 1 teaspoon soy sauce
- 1 teaspoon sea salt
- ½ teaspoon ground black pepper

1. Combine the ground pork, chicken, soy sauce, ground black pepper, garlic, basil, coriander, nutmeg, sea salt, and egg.
2. Add the coconut flour and mix the mixture well to combine.
3. Preheat your air fryer to 360°Fahrenheit.
4. Make medium-sized sausages with the ground meat mixture.
5. Spray the inside of the air fryer basket tray with the olive oil.
6. Place prepared sausages into the air fryer basket and place inside of air fryer.
7. Cook the sausages for 6-minutes.
8. Turn the sausages over and cook for 6-minutes more.
9. When the cook time is completed, let the sausages chill for a little bit. Serve warm.

PER SERVING

Calories: 156 | Total Fat: 7.5g | Carbs: 1.3g | Protein: 20.2g

Scrambled Pancake Hash

Prep time: 7 minutes | Cook time: 9 minutes | Serves 7

- 1 egg
- ¼ cup heavy cream
- 5 tablespoons butter
- 1 cup coconut flour
- 1 teaspoon ground ginger
- 1 teaspoon salt
- 1 tablespoon apple cider vinegar
- 1 teaspoon baking soda

1. Combine the salt, baking soda, ground ginger and flour in a mixing bowl.
2. In a separate bowl crack, the egg into it.
3. Add butter and heavy cream.
4. Mix well using a hand mixer.
5. Combine the liquid and dry mixtures and stir until smooth.
6. Preheat your air fryer to 400°Fahrenheit.
7. Pour the pancake mixture into the air fryer basket tray.
8. Cook the pancake hash for 4-minutes.
9. After this, scramble the pancake hash well and continue to cook for another 5-minutes more.
10. When dish is cooked, transfer it to serving plates, and serve hot!

PER SERVING

Calories: 178 | Total Fat: 13.3g | Carbs: 10.3g | Protein: 4.4g

Mozzarella Eggs

Prep time: 5 minutes | Cook time: 20 minutes |Serves 4

- 1 cup Mozzarella, shredded
- 4 eggs
- 1 teaspoon coconut oil, softened
- ½ teaspoon ground black pepper

1. Grease the air fryer basket with coconut oil and crack eggs inside.
2. Sprinkle the eggs with ground black pepper and Mozzarella.
3. Cook the meal at 360F for 20 minutes.

PER SERVING

Calories: 93 | Fat: 6.8 | Fiber: 0.1 | Carbs: 0.8 | Protein: 7.6

Almond Milk Bake

Prep time: 5 minutes | Cook time: 25 minutes |Serves 4

- 2 cups cauliflower, roughly chopped
- 2 ounces Monterey Jack cheese, shredded
- 4 eggs, beaten
- 1 cup organic almond milk
- 1 teaspoon dried oregano

1. In the mixing bowl, mix dried oregano with almond milk and eggs.
2. Pour the liquid in the air fryer basket and add cauliflower and cheese.
3. Close the lid and cook the meal at 350F for 25 minutes.

PER SERVING

Calories: 267 | Fat: 23.1 | Fiber: 2.7 | Carbs: 6.7 | Protein: 11.4

Baked Bacon Egg Cups

Prep time: 10 minutes | Cook time: 12 minutes | Serves 2

- 2 eggs
- 1 tablespoon chives, fresh, chopped
- ½ teaspoon paprika
- ½ teaspoon cayenne pepper
- 3-ounces cheddar cheese, shredded
- ½ teaspoon butter
- ¼ teaspoon salt
- 4-ounces bacon, cut into tiny pieces

1. Slice bacon into tiny pieces and sprinkle it with cayenne pepper, salt, and paprika.
2. Mix the chopped bacon.
3. Spread butter in bottom of ramekin dishes and beat the eggs there.
4. Add the chives and shredded cheese.
5. Add the chopped bacon over egg mixture in ramekin dishes.
6. Place the ramekins in your air fryer basket.
7. Preheat your air fryer to 360°Fahrenheit.
8. Place the air fryer basket in your air fryer and cook for 12-minutes.
9. When the cook time is completed, remove the ramekins from air fryer and serve warm.

PER SERVING

Calories: 553 | Total Fat: 43.3g | Carbs: 2.3g | Protein: 37.3g

Mascarpone Omelet

Prep time: 8 minutes | Cook time: 10 minutes | Serves 6

- 8 eggs, beaten
- ¼ cup mascarpone
- 1 teaspoon ground black pepper
- ½ teaspoon coconut oil

1. Mix eggs with mascarpone and ground black pepper.
2. Then grease the air fryer basket with coconut oil.
3. Add the egg mixture and cook the omelet for 10 minutes at 385F.

PER SERVING

Calories: 106 | Fat: 7.6 | Fiber: 0.1 | Carbs: 1 | Protein: 8.6

Chicken Bake

Prep time: 5 minutes | Cook time: 25 minutes | Serves 4

- 1 cup ground chicken
- ¼ cup Mozzarella, shredded
- 1 egg, beaten
- 1 teaspoon Italian seasonings
- 1 teaspoon coconut oil

1. In the mixing bowl, mix all ingredients until you get a homogenous mixture.
2. Then put it in the air fryer basket and bake at 370F for 25 minutes.

PER SERVING

Calories: 101 | Fat: 5.5 | Fiber: 0 | Carbs: 0.3 | Protein: 12

Rice Paper Bacon

Prep time: 10 minutes | Cook time: 30 minutes | Serves 4

- 4 pieces white rice paper,
- cut into 1-inch thick strips
- 2 tablespoons water

- 2 tablespoons liquid smoke
- 2 tablespoons cashew butter
- 3 tablespoons soy sauce or tamari

1. Preheat your air fryer to 350°Fahrenheit.
2. In a mixing bowl, add soy sauce, cashew butter, liquid smoke, and water, mix well.
3. Soak the rice paper in this mixture for 5 minutes.
4. Place the rice paper in air fryer and do not overlap pieces.
5. Air fry for 15-minutes or until crispy. Serve with steamed vegetables!

PER SERVING

Calories: 232 | Total Fat: 7.4g | Carbs: 6.2g | Protein: 7.3g

Italian Breakfast Frittata

Prep time: 5 minutes | Cook time: 10 minutes | Serves 2

- 4 cherry tomatoes, sliced into halves
- ½ Italian sausage, sliced
- ½ teaspoon Italian seasoning
- 3 eggs
- 2-ounces parmesan cheese, shredded
- 1 tablespoon parsley, chopped
- Salt and pepper to taste

1. Preheat your air fryer to 360°Fahrenheit.
2. Put the sausage and cherry tomatoes into baking dish and cook for 5-minutes.
3. Crack eggs into small bowl, add parsley, Italian seasoning and mix well by whisking.
4. Pour egg mixture over sausage and cherry tomatoes and place back into air fryer to cook for an additional 5-minutes. Serve warm.

PER SERVING

Calories: 242 | Total Fat: 11.2g | Carbs: 9.3g | Protein: 12.3g

Chapter 4

Bread, Pizza, and Pasta

Cranberry Bread

Prep time: 15 minutes | Cook time: 30 minutes | Serves 10

- Four eggs
- Three cups flour
- 2/3 cups sugar
- 2/3 cup vegetable oil
- ½ cup milk
- 1 teaspoon vanilla extract
- 2 teaspoons baking powder
- 2 cups fresh cranberries

1. In a bowl, add all the ingredients (except the cranberries) and stir until well combined.
2. Gently fold in the cranberries.
3. Place the mixture into a lightly greased baking pan evenly. Select the "Air Fry" mode. Press the Time button and set the cooking time to thirty mins. Then push the Temp button and rotate the dial to set the temperature at 320° F.
4. Press the Start button. When the unit beeps, open the lid.
5. Arrange the pan in the basket of the Air Fryer and insert it in the oven. Place the pan onto a wire rack and cook for about 10-15 mins.
6. Carefully invert the bread onto the wire rack to cool completely before slicing. Cut the bread into desired-sized slices.

PER SERVING

CALORIES: 436 | FAT: 16.9 G | CARBOHYDRATES:65.4 G

Cinnamon Zucchini Bread

Prep time: 10 minutes | Cook time: 40 minutes |Serves 12

- 2 cups coconut flour
- 2 teaspoons baking powder
- ¾ cup Erythritol
- ½ cup coconut oil, melted
- 1 teaspoon apple cider vinegar
- 1 teaspoon vanilla extract
- 3 eggs, beaten
- 1 zucchini, grated
- 1 teaspoon ground cinnamon

1. In the mixing bowl, mix coconut flour with baking powder, Erythritol, coconut oil, apple cider vinegar, vanilla extract, eggs, zucchini, and ground cinnamon.
2. Transfer the mixture in the air fryer basket and flatten it in the shape of the bread.
3. Cook the bread at 350F for 40 minutes.

PER SERVING

Calories: 179 | Fat: 12.2 | Fiber: 8.3 | Carbs: 14.6 | Protein: 4.3

Cheese Burgers

Prep time: 5 minutes | Cook time: 11 minutes | Serves 6

- 1 lb. ground beef
- 6 slices cheddar cheese
- Salt and pepper to taste

1. Preheat the air fryer to 350°Fahrenheit.
2. Season ground beef with pepper and salt.
3. Make six patties from the mixture and place them into air fryer basket.
4. Air fry patties for 10-minutes.
5. After 10-minutes, place cheese slices over patties and cook for another minute. Serve warm.

PER SERVING

Calories: 302 | Total Fat: 12.5g | Carbs: 12.2g | Protein: 16.2g

Cheese & Egg Breakfast Sandwich

Prep time: 5 minutes | Cook time: 6 minutes | Serves 1

- 1-2 eggs
- 1-2 slices of cheddar or Swiss cheese
- A bit of butter
- 1 roll sliced in half (your choice), Kaiser bun, English muffin, etc.

1. Butter your sliced roll on both sides.
2. Place the eggs in an oven-safe dish and whisk.
3. Add seasoning if you wish such as dill, chives, oregano, and salt.
4. Place the egg dish, roll and cheese into the air fryer.
5. Make sure the buttered sides of roll are facing upwards.
6. Set the air fryer to 390°Fahrenheit with a cook time of 6-minutes.
7. Remove the ingredients when cook time is completed by air fryer.
8. Place the egg and cheese between the pieces of roll and serve warm.
9. You might like to try adding slices of avocado and tomatoes to this breakfast sandwich!

PER SERVING

Calories: 212 | Total Fat: 11.2g | Carbs: 9.3g | Protein: 12.4g

Sweet Potato Black Bean Burgers

Prep time: 10 minutes | Cook time: 15 minutes | Serves 4

- 1 (15-ounce) can black beans, drained and rinsed
- 1 cup mashed sweet potato
- ½ teaspoon dried oregano
- ¼ teaspoon dried thyme
- ¼ teaspoon dried marjoram
- 1 garlic clove, minced
- ¼ teaspoon salt
- ¼ teaspoon black pepper
- 1 tablespoon lemon juice
- 1 cup cooked brown rice
- ¼ to ½ cup whole wheat bread crumbs
- 1 tablespoon olive oil

For Serving:
- Whole wheat buns or whole wheat pitas
- Plain Greek yogurt
- Avocado
- Lettuce
- Tomato
- Red onion

1. Preheat the air fryer to 380°F.
2. In a large bowl, use the back of a fork to mash the black beans until there are no large pieces left.
3. Add the mashed sweet potato, oregano, thyme, marjoram, garlic, salt, pepper, and lemon juice, and mix until well combined.
4. Stir in the cooked rice.
5. Add in ¼ cup of the whole wheat bread crumbs and stir. Check to see if the mixture is dry enough to form patties. If it seems too wet and loose, add an additional ¼ cup bread crumbs and stir.
6. Form the dough into 4 patties. Place them into the air fryer basket in a single layer, making sure that they don't touch each other.
7. Brush half of the olive oil onto the patties and bake for 5 minutes.
8. Flip the patties over, brush the other side with the remaining oil, and bake for an additional 4 to 5 minutes.

PER SERVING

Calories: 263 | Total Fat: 5g | Saturated Fat: 1g | Protein: 9g | Total Carbohydrates: 47g | Fiber: 8g | Sugar: 4g | Cholesterol: 0mg

Garlic Bread

Prep time:10 minutes |Cook time: 8 minutes |Serves 4

- 1 oz Mozzarella, shredded
- 2 tablespoons almond flour
- 1 teaspoon cream cheese
- ¼ teaspoon garlic powder
- ¼ teaspoon baking powder
- 1 egg, beaten
- 1 teaspoon coconut oil, melted
- ¼ teaspoon minced garlic
- 1 teaspoon dried dill
- 1 oz Provolone cheese, grated

1. In the mixing bowl mix up Mozzarella, almond flour, cream cheese, garlic powder, baking powder, egg, minced garlic, dried dill, and Provolone cheese.
2. When the mixture is homogenous, transfer it on the baking paper and spread it in the shape of the bread.
3. Sprinkle the garlic bread with coconut oil.
4. Preheat the air fryer to 400F.
5. Transfer the baking paper with garlic bread in the air fryer and cook for 8 minutes or until it is light brown.
6. When the garlic bread is cooked, cut it on 4 servings and place it in the serving plates.

PER SERVING

Calories 155| Fat 12.7| Fiber 1.6| Carbs 4| Protein 8.3

Greek Bread

Prep time:15 minutes |Cook time: 4 minutes |Serves 6

- 1 cup Mozzarella, shredded
- 2 tablespoons Greek yogurt
- 1 egg, beaten
- ½ teaspoon baking powder
- ½ cup almond flour
- 1 teaspoon butter, melted

1. In the glass bowl mix up Mozzarella and yogurt.
2. Microwave the mixture for 2 minutes.
3. After this, mix up baking powder, almond flour, and egg.
4. Combine together the almond flour mixture and melted Mozzarella mixture.
5. Stir it with the help of the spatula until smooth.
6. Refrigerate the dough for 10 minutes.
7. Then cut it on 6 pieces and roll up to get the flatbread pieces.
8. Air fryer the bread for 3 minutes at 400F.
9. Then brush it with melted butter and cook for 1 minute more or until the bread is light brown.

PER SERVING

Calories 43| Fat 3.4| Fiber 0.3| Carbs 0.9| Protein 2.8

Veggie Pizza

Prep time:10 minutes |Cook time: 15 minutes |Serves 4

- 8 bacon slices
- ¼ cup black olives, sliced
- ¼ cup scallions, sliced
- 1 green bell pepper, sliced
- 1 cup Mozzarella, shredded
- 1 tablespoon keto tomato sauce
- ½ teaspoon dried basil
- ½ teaspoon sesame oil

1. Line the air fryer pan with baking paper.
2. Then make the layer of the sliced bacon in the pan and sprinkle gently with sesame oil.
3. Preheat the air fryer to 400F.
4. Place the pan with the bacon in the air fryer basket and cook it for 9 minutes at 400F.
5. After this, sprinkle the bacon with keto tomato sauce and top with Mozzarella.
6. Then add bell pepper, spring onions, and black olives.
7. Sprinkle the pizza with dried basil and cook for 6 minutes at 400F.

PER SERVING

Calories 255| Fat 18.8| Fiber 0.9| Carbs 4.5| Protein 16.5

Cauliflower Pizza Crust

Prep time:10 minutes |Cook time: 6 minutes |Serves 6

- 1 cup cauliflower, shredded
- 1 egg
- ½ cup Cheddar cheese, shredded
- 1 teaspoon salt
- 1 teaspoon keto tomato sauce
- 1 tablespoon coconut flakes
- 1 teaspoon avocado oil
1. Crack the egg in the bowl and whisk it

gently.
2. Add shredded cauliflower, cheese, salt, tomato sauce, and coconut flakes.
3. Stir the mixture well.
4. Then put on the baking paper and roll up in the shape of the pizza crust.
5. Sprinkle it with avocado oil.
6. Preheat the air fryer to 400F.
7. Put the baking paper with pizza crust in the air fryer and cook it for 6 minutes.

PER SERVING

Calories 57| Fat 4.3| Fiber 0.5| Carbs 1.4| Protein 3.7

Meat Pizza

Prep time: 10 minutes | Cook time: 15 minutes |Serves 2

- 8 oz ground beef
- 1 tablespoon marinara sauce
- ½ teaspoon dried oregano
- 1/3 cup Cheddar cheese, shredded
- ½ teaspoon coconut oil, melted
- ¼ teaspoon dried cilantro

1. Mix ground beef with dried cilantro and dried oregano.
2. Brush the air fryer basket with coconut oil.
3. Make 2 flat balls from the ground beef and put them in the air fryer basket.
4. Top them with marinara sauce and Cheddar cheese.
5. Cook the pizza at 375F for 15 minutes.

PER SERVING

Calories: 304 | Fat: 14.7 | Fiber: 0.4 | Carbs: 1.6 | Protein: 39.3

Zucchini Pasta

Prep time:15 minutes |Cook time: 14 minutes |Serves 4

- ½ cup ground beef
- ¼ teaspoon salt
- ½ teaspoon chili flakes
- ¼ teaspoon dried dill
- 2 zucchinis, trimmed
- 2 tablespoons mascarpone
- 1 teaspoon olive oil
- ½ teaspoon ground black pepper
- Cooking spray

1. In the mixing bowl mix up ground beef, salt, chili flakes, and dill.
2. Then make the small meatballs.
3. Preheat the air fryer to 365F.
4. Spray the air fryer basket with cooking spray and place the meatballs inside in one layer.
5. Cook the meatballs for 12 minutes.
6. Shake them after 6 minutes of cooking to avoid burning.
7. Then remove the meatballs from the air fryer.
8. with the help of the spiralizer make the zucchini noodles and sprinkle them with olive oil and ground black pepper.
9. Place the zucchini noodles in the air fryer and cook them for 2 minutes at 400F.
10. Then mix up zucchini noodles and mascarpone and transfer them in the serving plates.
11. Top the noodles with cooked meatballs.

PER SERVING

Calories 145| Fat 8.8| Fiber 2.3| Carbs 7.5| Protein 10.7

Lemon Bread

Prep time: 15 minutes | Cook time: 30 minutes | Serves 10

- 3 cups all-purpose flour
- 3 tablespoons poppy seeds
- Three eggs
- 2 cups sugar
- 1½ cups milk
- 1½ teaspoon baking powder
- 1 teaspoon salt
- one cup vegetable oil
- 2 teaspoons fresh lemon juice
- 1 teaspoon pure vanilla extract
- 2 tablespoons lemon zest, grated

1. In a bowl, stir together the poppy seeds, flour, baking powder, and salt.
2. Add the eggs, oil, lemon juice, sugar, milk, and vanilla extract to another bowl and beat until well combined.
3. Add the flour mixture and toss until just combined. Fold in the lemon zest.
4. Place the mixture into a greased baking pan evenly. Select the "Air Fry" mode. Press the Time button and set the cooking time to thirty mins. Set the temperature to 310° F. Press the Start button.
5. When the unit beeps, open the lid.
6. Arrange the pan in the Air Fryer Basket and insert in the oven.
7. Place the pan on the top of a wire rack for about 10-15 mins.
8. Carefully, invert the bread onto the wire rack to cool completely before slicing.
9. Cut the bread into desired-sized slices.

PER SERVING

Calories: 533 | Fat: 25.4 g | Carbohydrates:71.8 g

Lemon Zucchini Bread

Prep time:10 minutes |Cook time: 40 minutes |Serves 12

- 2 cups almond flour
- 2 teaspoons baking powder
- ¾ cup swerve
- ½ cup coconut oil, melted
- 1 teaspoon lemon juice
- 1 teaspoon vanilla extract
- 3 eggs, whisked
- 1 cup zucchini, shredded
- 1 tablespoon lemon zest Cooking spray

1. In a bowl, mix all the ingredients except the cooking spray and stir well.
2. Grease a loaf pan that fits the air fryer with the cooking spray, line with parchment paper and pour the loaf mix inside.
3. Put the pan in the air fryer and cook at 330 degrees F for 40 minutes.
4. Cool down, slice and serve.

PER SERVING

Calories 143| Fat 11| Fiber 1| Carbs 3| Protein 3

Chicken English Muffin Sandwiches

Prep time: 20 minutes | Cook time:12 minutes |Serves 4

- 1 pound chicken breasts
- 1 tablespoon olive oil
- Sea salt and black pepper, to taste
- 4 slices cheddar cheese
- 4 teaspoons yellow mustard
- 4 English muffins, lightly toasted

1. Pat the chicken dry with kitchen towels. Toss the chicken breasts with the olive oil, salt, and pepper.
2. Cook the chicken at 380 degrees F for 12 minutes, turning them over halfway through the cooking time.
3. Shred the chicken using two forks and serve with cheese, mustard, and English muffin
4. Bon appétit!

PER SERVING

Calories: 439 | Fat: 21g | Carbohydrates: 26.2g | Protein: 35.3g | Sugars: 1g | Fiber: 2.8g

Pesto Pasta

Prep time:5 minutes |Cook time: 15 minutes |Serves 4

- 2 cups zucchinis, cut with a spiralizer
- Salt and black pepper to the taste
- 1 tablespoon olive oil
- ½ cup coconut cream
- 4 ounces mozzarella, shredded
- ¼ cup basil pesto

1. In a pan that fits your air fryer, mix the zucchini noodles with the pesto and the rest of the ingredients, toss, introduce the pan in the fryer and cook at 370 degrees F for 15 minutes.
2. Divide between plates and serve as a side dish.

PER SERVING

Calories 200| Fat 8| Fiber 2| Carbs 4| Protein 10

Spinach and Chicken Pita Pizza

Prep time: 5 minutes | Cook time: 7 minutes | Serves 1

- 1 whole wheat pita
- 1 tablespoon olive oil
- 1 garlic clove, minced
- ¼ teaspoon red pepper flakes
- ½ cup baby spinach
- ¼ sliced red onion
- ½ cup cooked chicken breast, cubed
- ¼ cup feta cheese, crumbled

1. Preheat the air fryer to 380°F.
2. Brush the top of the pita with the olive oil and top with the garlic, red pepper flakes, spinach, onion, chicken, and feta.
3. Place the pizza into the air fryer basket and cook for 7 minutes.
4. Remove the pizza from the air fryer. Cut into 2 to 4 pieces and enjoy!

PER SERVING

Calories: 519 | Total Fat: 26g | Saturated Fat: 8g | Protein: 34g | Total Carbohydrates: 40g | Fiber: 5g | Sugar: 3g | Cholesterol: 93mg

Shrimp Spaghetti

Prep time: 10 minutes | Cook time: 15 minutes | Serves 4

- 5 ounces spaghetti, cooked
- 8 ounces shrimp, peeled and deveined
- 1 tablespoon butter, melted
- 2 tablespoons olive oil
- Salt and black pepper to taste
- Five garlic cloves, minced
- 1 teaspoon chili powder

1. Put 1 tablespoon of the olive oil, along with the butter, in your Air Fryer.
2. Preheat the oven to 350° F, add the shrimp and cook for ten minutes.
3. Add all other ingredients, including the remaining 1 tablespoon of oil, stir, and cook for five minutes more.

PER SERVING

Calories: 270.3 | Fat: 7.3 g | Carbohydrates:14.5 g

Chapter 5

Poultry

Herb-Roasted Beef Tips with Onions

Prep time: 5 minutes | Cook time: 10 minutes | Serves 4

- 1 pound rib eye steak, cubed
- 2 garlic cloves, minced
- 2 tablespoons olive oil
- 1 tablespoon fresh oregano
- 1 teaspoon salt
- ½ teaspoon black pepper
- 1 yellow onion, thinly sliced

1. Preheat the air fryer to 380°F.
2. In a medium bowl, combine the steak, garlic, olive oil, oregano, salt, pepper, and onion. Mix until all of the beef and onion are well coated.
3. Put the seasoned steak mixture into the air fryer basket. Roast for 5 minutes. Stir and roast for 5 minutes more.
4. Let rest for 5 minutes before serving with some favorite sides.

PER SERVING

Calories: 380 | Total Fat: 28g | Saturated Fat: 11g | Protein: 28g | Total Carbohydrates: 3g | Fiber: 0g | Sugar: 1g | Cholesterol: 88mg

Ham and Cheese Stuffed Chicken

Prep time: 25 minutes | Cook time:22 minutes |Serves 4

- 1 pound chicken breasts, skinless, boneless and cut into 4 slices
- 4 ounces goat cheese, crumbled
- 4 ounces ham, chopped
- 1 egg
- 1/4 cup all-purpose flour
- 1/4 cup parmesan cheese, grated
- 1/2 teaspoon onion powder
- 1/2 teaspoon garlic powder

1. Flatten the chicken breasts with a mallet.
2. Stuff each piece of chicken with cheese and ham. Roll them up and secure with toothpicks.
3. In a shallow bowl, mix the remaining ingredients until well combined. Dip the chicken rolls into the egg/flour mixture.
4. Place the stuffed chicken in the Air Fryer cooking basket. Cook the stuffed chicken breasts at 400 degrees F for about 22 minutes, turning them over halfway through the cooking time.
5. Bon appétit!

PER SERVING

Calories: 486 | Fat: 32.3g | Carbohydrates: 7.9g | Protein: 39.3g | Sugars: 0.8g | Fiber: 0.2g

Ranch Chicken Wings

Prep time: 25 minutes | Cook time: 17 minutes |Serves 3

- 1 pound chicken wings, boneless
- 2 tablespoons olive oil
- 1 teaspoon Ranch seasoning mix
- Kosher salt and ground black pepper, to taste

1. Pat the chicken dry with kitchen towels. Toss the chicken with the remaining ingredients.
2. Cook the chicken wings at 380 degrees F for 22 minutes, turning them over halfway through the cooking time.
3. Bon appétit!

PER SERVING

Calories: 273 | Fat: 14.3g | Carbohydrates: 0.5g | Protein: 33.2g | Sugars: 0.4g | Fiber: 0.5g

Chicken Wrapped In Bacon

Prep time: 5 minutes | Cook time: 15 minutes | Serves 6

- 6 slices of bacon
- 1 small chicken breast
- 1 tablespoon garlic, minced
- Soft cheese

1. Chop up chicken breast into bite-sized pieces.
2. Lay out bacon slices and spread cheese on top.
3. Place chicken on top of cheese and roll up.
4. Secure with a cocktail stick.
5. Place wrapped chicken pieces in air fryer and cooked for 15-minutes at 350°Fahrenheit.

PER SERVING

Calories: 296 | Total Fat: 11.8g | Carbs: 8.7g | Protein: 15.2g

Tandoori Chicken with Mint Yogurt

Prep time: 5 minutes | Cook time: 20 minutes | Serves 4

- 2-ounces of chicken breast
- 2 tablespoons tandoori paste, divided
- 4 tablespoons + ¾ cup
- Greek yogurt, divided
- 3 sprigs of mint, minced
- Salt and pepper to taste
- 1 tablespoon olive oil
- 2 cups cooked basmati rice
- Mint leaves for garnishing

1. Combine 1 tablespoon of tandoori paste and 2 tablespoons of yogurt in a bowl.
2. Coat the chicken breast with mixture.
3. Marinate for 2-hours in the fridge.
4. Preheat your air fryer to 360°Fahrenheit

for 5-minutes.

5. Set air fryer timer to 15-minutes and place the chicken inside.
6. Prepare the mint yogurt sauce by mixing the minced mint with 2 tablespoons of yogurt.
7. Season with salt and pepper and stir well.
8. Prepare tandoori sauce: heat the olive oil in a pan over medium heat and sauté 1 tablespoon tandoori paste for 3-minutes.
9. Add remaining ¾ cup of yogurt and sauté for another 2-minutes.
10. Slice the chicken breast and serve with basmati rice.
11. Cover meat with tandoori sauce and mint yogurt sauce on top.
12. Garnish with mint leaves.

PER SERVING

Calories: 289 | Total Fat: 11.3g | Carbs: 9.7g | Protein: 14.8g

Greek Chicken Salad

Prep time: 20 minutes | Cook time:12 minutes |Serves 4

- 1 pound chicken breasts, boneless, skinless
- 1 red onion, thinly sliced
- 1 bell pepper, sliced
- 4 Kalamata olives, pitted and minced
- 1 small Greek cucumber, grated and squeezed
- 4 tablespoons Greek yogurt
- 4 tablespoons mayonnaise
- 1 tablespoon fresh lemon juice
- Coarse sea salt and red pepper flakes, to taste

1. Pat the chicken dry with paper towels. Place the chicken breasts in a lightly oiled Air Fryer basket.
2. Cook the chicken at 380 degrees F for 12 minutes, turning them over halfway through the cooking time.
3. Chop the chicken breasts and transfer it to a salad bowl | add in the remaining ingredients and toss to combine well.
4. Serve well-chilled and enjoy!

PER SERVING

Calories: 314 | Fat: 21g | Carbohydrates: 3.2g | Protein: 24.8g | Sugars: 2.1g | Fiber: 0.6g

Bacon Wrapped Herb Chicken

Prep time: 5 minutes | Cook time: 15 minutes | Serves 6

- 1 chicken breast, cut into 6 pieces
- 6 slices of bacon
- ½ teaspoon basil, dried
- ½ teaspoon parsley, dried
- ½ teaspoon paprika
- Salt and pepper to taste
- 1 tablespoon soft cheese

1. In a bowl, mix basil, parsley, salt, pepper, and paprika.
2. Place the bacon slices on a dish and spread them with soft cheese.
3. Place the chicken pieces into basil mix and cover with seasoning.
4. Place the chicken pieces on top of bacon slices.
5. Roll up and secure with toothpick.
6. Place into air fryer and cook at 350°Fahrenheit and cook for 15-minutes.

PER SERVING

Calories: 298 | Total Fat: 11.4g | Carbs: 8.9g | Protein: 13.6g

Chicken Cutlets with Broccoli

Prep time: 15 minutes | Cook time:6 minutes |Serves 4

- 1 pound chicken cutlets
- 1 pound broccoli florets
- 1 tablespoon olive oil
- Sea salt and ground black pepper, to taste

1. Pat the chicken dry with kitchen towels. Place the chicken cutlets in a lightly greased Air Fryer basket.
2. Cook the chicken cutlets at 380 degrees F for 6 minutes, turning them over halfway through the cooking time.
3. Turn the heat to 400 degrees F and add in the remaining ingredients. Continue to cook for 6 minutes more
4. Bon appétit!

PER SERVING

Calories: 313 |Fat: 20.8g | Carbohydrates: 7.5g | Protein: 24.5g | Sugars: 1.9g | Fiber: 2g

Lemon Chicken & Peppercorns

Prep time: 5 minutes | Cook time: 15 minutes | Serves 1

- 1 chicken breast
- Salt and pepper to taste
- 1 tablespoon chicken seasoning
- Handful of peppercorns
- 1 lemon juice
- 1 teaspoon garlic, minced

1. Preheat your air fryer to 350°Fahrenheit.
2. Season the chicken with salt and pepper.
3. Rub chicken seasoning all over the chicken.
4. Place the seasoned chicken onto aluminum foil sheet.
5. Add garlic, lemon juice, black peppercorns on top of chicken and seal the foil.
6. Place chicken in air fryer and cook for 15-minutes.

PER SERVING

Calories: 300 | Total Fat: 10.8g | Carbs: 9.4g | Protein: 14.6g

Buttermilk Chicken

Prep time: 5 minutes | Cook time: 18 minutes | Serves 4

- 2 lbs. chicken thighs
- 2 teaspoons black pepper
- 1 teaspoon salt
- 1 tablespoon garlic powder
- 1 teaspoon cayenne pepper
- 1 tablespoon baking powder
- 2 cups almond flour
- 2 cups buttermilk
- 1 tablespoon paprika

1. Rinse the chicken thighs then pat dry.
2. Add black pepper, paprika, and salt in a bowl.
3. Toss the chicken pieces in paprika mixture.
4. Pour buttermilk over chicken until coated.
5. Place in the fridge for about 6-hours.
6. Preheat your air fryer to 355°Fahrenheit.
7. Use a different bowl to mix flour, baking powder, salt, garlic powder and black pepper.
8. Coat chicken thighs in seasoned flour.
9. Remove any excess flour then place on a plate.
10. Arrange the chicken in one layer on fryer basket and place basket inside air fryer and cook for 8-minutes.
11. Pull out the tray and turn chicken pieces over and cook for an additional 10-minutes.

PER SERVING

Calories: 292 | Total Fat: 11.3g | Carbs: 9.2g | Protein: 14.8g

Turkey Meatballs

Prep time: 10 Minutes | Cook time: 20 minutes | Serves 6

- 1 lb ground turkey
- Two eggs, lightly beaten
- 1 tablespoon basil, chopped
- 1/3 cup coconut flour
- 1 tablespoon dried onion flakes
- 2 cups zucchini, grated
- 1 teaspoon dried oregano
- 1 tablespoon garlic, minced
- 1 teaspoon cumin
- 1 tablespoon nutritional yeast
- Salt and Pepper

1. Select "Bake" to your Air Fryer and preheat to 390 degrees F for twenty minutes.
2. Add all ingredients into a bowl and mix until well combined.
3. Make small balls from the meat mixture, place them on a roasting pan and bake for twenty minutes.

PER SERVING

Calories: 213 | Fat: 11.7 g | Carbohydrates:7.9 g | Protein: 23.9 g

Creamed Chicken Salad

Prep time: 20 minutes | Cook time:12 minutes |Serves 4

- 1 pound chicken breasts, skinless and boneless
- 1/4 cup mayonnaise
- 1/4 cup sour cream
- 1 tablespoon lemon juice
- Sea salt and ground black pepper
- 1/2 cup celery, chopped

1. Pat the chicken dry with paper towels. Place the chicken in a lightly oiled cooking basket.
2. Cook the chicken breasts at 380 degrees F for 12 minutes, turning them over halfway through the cooking time.
3. Shred the chicken breasts using two forks | transfer it to a salad bowl and add in the remaining ingredients.
4. Toss to combine and serve well chilled. Bon appétit!

PER SERVING

Calories: 315 | Fat: 23g | Carbohydrates: 2.8g | Protein: 24.5g | Sugars: 0.9g | Fiber: 0.4g

Coconut & Turmeric Air-Fried Chicken

Prep time: 5 minutes | Cook time: 25 minutes | Serves 2

- 3 pieces whole chicken legs
- ¼ cup pure coconut paste
- ¾ tablespoon salt
- ¼ cup ginger
- 4 teaspoons turmeric

1. Blend all the ingredients, except chicken in a bowl.
2. Cut slits on chicken legs especially on thick parts.
3. Season chicken well.
4. Preheat your air fryer to 375°Fahrenheit.
5. Air fry chicken for 25-minutes and halfway through the cook time flip the chicken over.

PER SERVING

Calories: 298 | Total Fat: 11.5g | Carbs: 9.3g | Protein: 14.3g

Chapter 6

Beef, Pork and Lamb

Garlicky Roast Beef

Prep time: 4 hours | Cook time:55 minutes |Serves 4

- 1 ½ pounds eye round roast
- 4 cloves garlic, peeled and thinly sliced
- 2 tablespoons olive oil
- Kosher salt and ground black pepper, to taste

1. Pierce the beef with a sharp knife and insert the garlic slices into the holes.
2. Toss the meat with the oil, salt, and black pepper and transfer it to the Air Fryer cooking basket.
3. Cook the roast beef at 390 degrees F for 55 minutes, turning it over halfway through the cooking time.
4. Enjoy!

PER SERVING

Calories: 301 | Fat: 11.5g | Carbohydrates: 3g | Protein: 38.1g | Sugars: 0.8g | Fiber: 0.4g

Parmesan Filet Mignon

Prep time: 15 minutes | Cook time:14 minutes |Serves 4

- 1 pound filet mignon
- Sea salt and ground black pepper, to season
- 1 teaspoon red pepper flakes
- 1 teaspoon rosemary, finely chopped
- 2 tablespoons olive oil
- 1 cup parmesan cheese, preferably freshly grated

1. Toss the filet mignon with the salt, black pepper, red pepper, rosemary, and olive oil place the filet mignon in the Air Fryer cooking basket.
2. Cook the filet mignon at 400 degrees F for 14 minutes, turning it over halfway through the cooking time.

PER SERVING

Calories: 382 | Fat: 26.5g | Carbohydrates: 4.9g | Protein: 31.1g | Sugars: 0.6g | Fiber: 0.2g

Roasted Rack of Lamb with Macadamia Crust

Prep time: 5 minutes | Cook time: 35 minutes | Serves 4

- 1 garlic clove, minced
- 1 1/3 lbs.
- rack of lamb
- 1 tablespoon olive oil
- Salt and pepper to taste

Macadamia Crust:
- 3-ounces macadamia nuts, raw and unsalted
- 1 egg, beaten
- 1 tablespoon fresh rosemary, chopped
- 1 tablespoon breadcrumbs

1. In a small mixing bowl, mix garlic and olive oil.
2. Brush all over lamb and season with salt and pepper.
3. In your food processor, chop macadamia nuts and mix with breadcrumbs and rosemary.
4. Be careful not to make the nuts into a paste.
5. Stir in egg.
6. Coat lamb with nut mixture.
7. Preheat your air fryer to 220°Fahrenheit.
8. Place the lamb in air fryer and cook for 30-minutes.
9. Raise the temperature to 390°Fahrenheit and cook for an additional 5-minutes.
10. Remove the meat, cover it loosely with foil for 10-minutes. Serve warm.

PER SERVING

Calories: 306 | Total Fat: 11.4g | Carbs: 10.7g | Protein: 16.5g

Italian Pulled Pork Ragu

Prep time: 70 minutes | Cook time:70 minutes |Serves 5

- 2 pounds beef shoulder
- Kosher salt and ground black pepper, to taste
- 2 garlic cloves, minced
- 1 tablespoon Italian seasoning mix

1. Toss the beef shoulder with the remaining ingredients | now, place the beef shoulder in the Air Fryer cooking basket.
2. Cook the beef shoulder at 390 degrees F for 15 minutes, turn the beef shoulder over and reduce the temperature to 360 degrees F.
3. Continue to cook the beef shoulder for approximately 55 minutes or until cooked through.
4. Shred the beef shoulder with two forks and serve with toppings of choice. Bon appétit!

PER SERVING

Calories: 259 | Fat: 10.9g | Carbohydrates: 2.5g | Protein: 37g | Sugars: 0.6g | Fiber: 0.4g

Air-Fried Lamb Chops

Prep time: 5 minutes | Cook time: 32 minutes | Serves 4

- 1 tablespoon + 2 tablespoons
- olive oil, divided
- 4 lamb chops
- Pinch of black pepper
- 1 tablespoon dried thyme
- 1 garlic clove
-

1. Preheat your air fryer to 390°Fahrenheit.
2. Cook the garlic with 1 teaspoon olive oil for 10-minutes in air fryer.
3. Combine thyme and pepper with rest of olive oil.
4. Squeeze the roasted garlic and stir into thyme and oil mixture.
5. Brush mixture over lamb chops.
6. Cook for 12-minutes in air fryer.

PER SERVING

Calories: 312 | Total Fat: 12.3g | Carbs: 10.2g | Protein: 16.5g

Pork Loin with Potatoes & Herbs

Prep time: 5 minutes | Cook time: 25 minutes | Serves 2

- 2 lbs. pork loin
- ½ teaspoon garlic powder
- ½ teaspoon red pepper flakes
- ½ teaspoon black pepper
- 2 large potatoes, chunked

7. Sprinkle the pork loin with garlic powder, red pepper flakes, parsley, salt, and pepper.
8. Preheat your air fryer to 370°Fahrenheit and place pork loin and potatoes to one side in basket of air fryer.
9. Cook for 25-minutes.
10. Remove the pork loin and potatoes from air fryer.
11. Allow pork loin to cool before slicing and enjoy!

PER SERVING

Calories: 268 | Total Fat: 12.3g | Carbs: 11.6g | Protein: 16.2g

Summer Pork Skewers

Prep time: 20 minutes | Cook time:15 minutes |Serves 4

- 1 pound pork tenderloin, cubed
- 1 pound bell peppers, diced
- 1 pound eggplant, diced
- 1 tablespoon olive oil
- 1 tablespoon parsley, chopped
- 1 tablespoon cilantro, chopped
- Sea salt and ground black pepper, to taste

1. Toss all ingredients in a mixing bowl until well coated on all sides.
2. Thread the ingredients onto skewers and place them in the Air Fryer cooking basket.
3. Then, cook the skewers at 400 degrees F for approximately 15 minutes, turning them over halfway through the cooking time.
4. Bon appétit!

PER SERVING

Calories: 344 | Fat: 16.3g | Carbohydrates: 18g | Protein: 32.6g | Sugars: 10.1g | Fiber: 5.3g

Beef Sausage with Baby Potatoes

Prep time: 20 minutes | Cook time: 15 minutes |Serves 4

- 8 baby potatoes, scrubbed and halved
- 4 smoked beef sausages
- 1 teaspoon Italian seasoning mix

1. Toss all ingredients in a lightly oiled Air Fryer cooking basket.
2. Cook the sausage and potatoes at 400 degrees F for 15 minutes, tossing the basket halfway through the cooking time.
3. Serve warm and enjoy!

PER SERVING

Calories: 625 | Fat: 33g | Carbohydrates: 62.1g | Protein: 20.7g | Sugars: 2.6g | Fiber: 7.4g

Italian-Style Pork Center Cut

Prep time: 55 minutes | Cook time:55 minutes |Serves 5

- 2 pounds pork center cut
- 2 tablespoons olive oil
- 1 tablespoon Italian herb mix
- 1 teaspoon red pepper flakes, crushed
- Sea salt and freshly ground black pepper, to taste

1. Toss all ingredients in a lightly greased Air Fryer cooking basket.
2. Cook the pork at 360 degrees F for 55 minutes, turning it over halfway through the cooking time.
3. Serve warm and enjoy!

PER SERVING

Calories: 356 | Fat: 21.7g |Carbohydrates: 0.1g | Protein: 37.5g | Sugars: 0.1g | Fiber: 0.1g

BBQ Pork Ribs

Prep time: 40 minutes | Cook time:35 minutes |Serves 4

- 1 ½ pound baby back ribs
- 2 tablespoons olive oil
- 1 teaspoon smoked paprika
- 1 teaspoon garlic powder
- 1 teaspoon onion powder
- 1/2 teaspoon ground cumin
- 1 teaspoon mustard powder
- 1 teaspoon dried thyme
- Coarse sea salt and freshly cracked black pepper, to season

1. Toss all ingredients in a lightly greased Air Fryer cooking basket.
2. Cook the pork ribs at 350 degrees F for 35 minutes, turning them over halfway through the cooking time.
3. Bon appétit!

PER SERVING

Calories: 440 | Fat: 33.3g | Carbohydrates: 1.8g | Protein: 33.7g | Sugars: 0.1g | Fiber: 0.4g

Pumpkin & Pork Empanadas

Prep time: 10 minutes | Cook time: 30 minutes | Serves 4

- 2 tablespoons olive oil
- 1 package of 10 empanada discs
- Black pepper to taste
- 1 teaspoon salt
- ½ teaspoon dried thyme
- ½ teaspoon cinnamon
- 1 red chili pepper, minced
- 3 tablespoons water
- 1 ½ cups pumpkin puree
- 1 lb. ground pork
- ½ onion, diced

1. In a saucepan warm some olive oil.
2. Fry the onions and pork for about 5-minutes.
3. Pour away the fat, then add pumpkin, chili, cinnamon, water, thyme, salt, and pepper.
4. Stir well.
5. Cook for 10-minutes to allow flavors to blend.
6. Set aside to cool.
7. Open the packet of empanada discs and spread them out over your countertop.
8. Add a couple of tablespoons of filling to each, brush the edges with water and then fold towards center, to form a Cornish pasty shape.
9. Brush olive oil and repeat with the rest.
10. Place the empanadas inside of wire basket in your air fryer and cook at 370°Fahrenheit for 15-minutes.
11. Make sure to check often and turn as required. Serve and enjoy!

PER SERVING

Calories: 262 | Total Fat: 11.5g | Carbs: 9.7g | Protein: 15.2g

Crumbed Pork & Semi-Dried Tomato Pesto

Prep time: 15 minutes | Cook time: 20 minutes |
Serves 2

- ½ cup milk
- 1 egg
- 1 cup breadcrumbs
- 1 tablespoon parmesan cheese, grated
- ¼ bunch of thyme, chopped
- 1 teaspoon pine nuts
- ¼ cup semi-dried tomatoes
- ½ cup almond flour
- 2 pork cutlets
- 1 lemon, zested
- Sea salt and black pepper to taste
- 6 basil leaves
- 1 tablespoon olive oil

1. Combine and whisk milk and egg in a bowl, then set aside.
2. Mix in another bowl, breadcrumbs, parmesan, thyme, lemon zest, salt, and pepper.
3. Add flour to another bowl.
4. Dip pork cutlet in flour, then into egg and milk mixture, and finally into breadcrumb mixture.
5. Preheat air fryer to 360°Fahrenheit.
6. Spray basket with cooking spray.
7. Set the air fryer timer to 20-minutes.
8. Place pork inside of basket and cook until golden and crisp.
9. Prepare the pesto: add the tomatoes, pine nuts, olive oil, and basil leaves into food processor.
10. Blend for 20-seconds.
11. When the pork is ready, serve with pesto and a salad of your choice.

PER SERVING

Calories: 264 | Total Fat: 13.2g | Carbs: 11.7g | Protein: 16.3g

Rosemary Pork Shoulder Chops

Prep time: 20 minutes | Cook time:15 minutes
|Serves 4

- 1 ½ pounds pork shoulder chops
- 2 tablespoons olive oil
- Kosher salt and ground black pepper, to taste
- 2 sprigs rosemary, leaves picked and chopped
- 1 teaspoon garlic, pressed

1. Toss all ingredients in a lightly greased Air Fryer cooking basket.
2. Cook the pork shoulder chops at 400 degrees F for 15 minutes, turning them over halfway through the cooking time.
3. Bon appétit!

PER SERVING

Calories: 354 | Fat: 22.3g | Carbohydrates: 1.5g | Protein: 35.7g | Sugars: 0.5g | Fiber: 0.3g

Butter and Allspice Coulotte Roast

Prep time: 55 minutes | Cook time:55 minutes
|Serves 5

- 2 pounds Coulotte roast
- 2 tablespoons butter
- Kosher salt and ground black pepper, to taste
- 1 teaspoon ground allspice
- 1 teaspoon garlic, minced

1. Toss the beef with the remaining ingredients | place the beef in the Air Fryer cooking basket.
2. Cook the beef at 390 degrees F for 55 minutes, turning it over halfway through the cooking time.
3. Enjoy!

PER SERVING

Calories: 300 | Fat: 15.5g | Carbohydrates: 1.3g | Protein: 37.1g | Sugars: 0.4g | Fiber: 0.2g

Chapter 7

Fish and Seafood

Italian Fish Fingers

Prep time: 15 minutes | Cook time:10 minutes |Serves 4

- 1/2 cup all-purpose flour
- Sea salt and ground black pepper
- 1 teaspoon cayenne pepper
- 1/2 teaspoon onion powder
- 1 tablespoon Italian parsley, chopped
- 1 teaspoon garlic powder
- 1 egg, whisked
- 1/2 cup Pecorino Romano cheese, grated
- 1 pound monkfish, sliced into strips

1. In a shallow bowl, mix the flour, spices, egg, and cheese. Dip the fish strips in the batter until they are well coated on all sides.
2. Arrange the fish strips in the Air Fryer cooking basket.
3. Cook the fish strips at 400 degrees F for about 10 minutes, shaking the basket halfway through the cooking time.
4. Bon appétit!

PER SERVING

Calories: 218 | Fat: 6.4g | Carbohydrates: 14.6g | Protein: 23.8g | Sugars: 0.8g | Fiber: 0.9g

Mediterranean-Pita Wraps

Prep time: 15 minutes | Cook time:14 minutes |Serves 4

- 1 pound mackerel fish fillets
- 2 tablespoons olive oil
- 1 tablespoon Mediterranean seasoning mix
- 1/2 teaspoon chili powder
- Sea salt and freshly ground black pepper, to taste
- 2 ounces Feta cheese, crumbled
- 4 (6-1/2 inch) tortillas

1. Toss the fish fillets with the olive oil | place them in a lightly oiled Air Fryer cooking basket.

2. Cook the fish fillets at 400 degrees F for about 14 minutes, turning them over halfway through the cooking time.
3. Assemble your pitas with the chopped fish and remaining ingredients and serve warm. Bon appétit!

PER SERVING

Calories: 366 | Fat: 16.3g | Carbohydrates: 16.4g | Protein: 38.1g | Sugars: 2.9g | Fiber: 3.7g

Salmon with Creamy Zucchini

Prep time: 15 minutes | Cook time: 10 minutes | Serves 2

- 2 (6-ounce) salmon fillets, skin on
- Salt and pepper to taste
- 1 teaspoon olive oil

Courgette:
- 2 large zucchinis, trimmed and spiralized
- 1 avocado, peeled and chopped
- Small handful of parsley, chopped
- ½ garlic clove, minced
- Small handful cherry tomatoes, halved
- Small handful of black olives, chopped
- 2 tablespoons pine nuts, toasted

1. Preheat your air fryer to 350°Fahrenheit.
2. Brush salmon with olive oil and season with salt and pepper.
3. Place salmon in air fryer and cook for 10-minutes.
4. Blend the avocado, garlic, and parsley in a food processor until smooth.
5. Toss in a bowl with zucchini, olives, and tomatoes.
6. Divide vegetables between two plates, top each portion with salmon fillet, sprinkle with pine nuts, and serve.

PER SERVING

Calories: 302 | Total Fat: 9.3g | Carbs: 7.8g | Protein: 15.7g

Greek Pesto Salmon

Prep time: 10 minutes | Cook time: 30 minutes |
Serves 4

- Four salmon fillets
- 1/2 cup pesto
- One onion, chopped
- 2 cups grape tomatoes, halved
- 1/2 cup feta cheese, crumbled

1. Line a baking pan with foil and set aside.
2. Place salmon fillet in the baking pan and top with tomatoes, pesto, onion, and cheese.
3. Set the Air Fryer to Bake and cook at 350 degrees F for twenty minutes.

PER SERVING

CALORIES: 447 | FAT: 28 G | CARBOHY-
DRATES:8 G | PROTEIN: 41 G

Sesame Shrimp

Prep time: 15 minutes | Cook time: 12 minutes |
Serves 4

- 1 lb. shrimp; peeled and deveined
- 1 tbsp. olive oil
- 1 tbsp. Sesame seeds, toasted
- ½ tsp. Italian seasoning
- A pinch of salt and pepper

1. Take a bowl and mix the shrimp with the rest of the ingredients and stir well.
2. Put the shrimp in the Air Fryer's basket, cook at 370 degrees F for twelve minutes.

PER SERVING

CALORIES:199 | FAT: 11 G | CARBOHYDRATES:
4 G | PROTEIN: 11 G

Black Cod with Grapes, Pecans, Fennel & Kale

Prep time: 5 minutes | Cook time: 15 minutes |
Serves 2

- 2 fillets black cod (8-ounces)
- 3 cups kale, minced
- 2 teaspoons white balsamic vinegar
- ½ cup pecans
- 1 cup grapes, halved
- 1 small bulb fennel, cut into inch-thick slices
- 4 tablespoons extra-virgin olive oil
- Salt and black pepper to taste

1. Preheat your air fryer to 400°Fahrenheit.
2. Use salt and pepper to season your fish fillets.
3. Drizzle with 1 teaspoon of olive oil.
4. Place the fish inside of air fryer with the skin side down and cook for 10-minutes.
5. Take the fish out and cover loosely with aluminum foil.
6. Combine fennel, pecans, and grapes.
7. Pour 2 tablespoons of olive oil and season with salt and pepper.
8. Add to the air fryer basket.
9. Cook for an additional 5-minutes.
10. In a bowl combine minced kale and cooked grapes, fennel and pecans.
11. Cover ingredients with balsamic vinegar and remaining 1 tablespoon of olive oil.
12. Toss gently.
13. Serve fish with sauce and enjoy!

PER SERVING

Calories: 289 | Total Fat: 9.2g | Carbs: 8.6g |
Protein: 16.3g

Butter Cilantro Shrimp

Prep time: 10 minutes | Cook time:8 minutes |Serves 4

- 1 pound jumbo shrimp
- 2 tablespoons butter, at room temperature
- Coarse sea salt and lemon pepper, to taste
- 2 tablespoons fresh cilantro, chopped
- 2 tablespoons fresh chives, chopped
- 2 garlic cloves, crushed

1. Toss all ingredients in a lightly greased Air Fryer cooking basket.
2. Cook the shrimp at 400 degrees F for 8 minutes, tossing the basket halfway through the cooking time.
3. Bon appétit!

PER SERVING

Calories: 160 |Fat: 6.3g | Carbohydrates: 0.6g | Protein: 23.1g |Sugars: 0.1g | Fiber: 0.2g

Salmon Patties

Prep time: 10 minutes | Cook time: 10 minutes | Serves 2

- 3 large russet potatoes, boiled, mashed
- 1 salmon fillet
- 1 egg
- Breadcrumbs
- 2 tablespoons olive oil
- Parsley, fresh, chopped
- Handful of parboiled vegetables
- ½ teaspoon dill
- Salt and pepper to taste

1. Peel, chop, and mash cooked potatoes.
2. Set aside.
3. Preheat your air fryer for 5-minutes at 355°Fahrenheit.
4. Air fry salmon for five minutes.
5. Use a fork to flake salmon then set aside.
6. Add vegetables, parsley, flaked salmon, dill, salt, and pepper to mashed potatoes.

7. Add egg and combine.
8. Shape the mixture into six patties.
9. Cover with breadcrumbs.
10. Cook in air fryer for 10-minutes.

PER SERVING

Calories: 297 | Total Fat: 8.5g | Carbs: 7.2g | Protein: 14.7g

Shrimp and Swiss Chard Bowl

Prep time: 10 minutes | Cook time: 10 minutes |Serves 4

- 1-pound shrimp, peeled and deveined
- ½ teaspoon smoked paprika
- ½ cup Swiss chard, chopped
- 2 tablespoons apple cider vinegar
- 1 tablespoon coconut oil
- ¼ cup heavy cream

1. Mix shrimps with smoked paprika and apple cider vinegar.
2. Put the shrimps in the air fryer and add coconut oil.
3. Cook the shrimps at 350F for 10 minutes.
4. Then mix cooked shrimps with remaining ingredients and carefully mix.

PER SERVING

Calories: 193 | Fat: 8.1 | Fiber: 0.2 | Carbs: 2.3 | Protein: 26.1

Grilled Salmon with Capers & Dill

Prep time: 15 minutes | Cook time: 8 minutes | Serves 2

- 1 teaspoon capers, chopped
- 2 sprigs dill, chopped
- 1 lemon zest
- 1 tablespoon olive oil
- 4 slices lemon (optional)
- 11-ounce salmon fillet

Dressing:
5 capers, chopped
1 sprig dill, chopped
2 tablespoons plain yogurt
Pinch of lemon zest
Salt and black pepper to taste

1. Preheat your air fryer to 400°Fahrenheit.
2. Mix dill, capers, lemon zest, olive oil and salt in a bowl.
3. Cover the salmon with this mixture.
4. Cook salmon for 8-minutes.
5. Combine the dressing ingredients in another bowl.
6. When salmon is cooked, place on serving plate and drizzle dressing over it.
7. Place lemon slices at the side of the plate and serve.

PER SERVING

Calories: 300 | Total Fat: 8.9g | Carbs: 7.3g | Protein: 16.2g

Salmon with Dill Sauce

Prep time: 15 minutes | Cook time: 23 minutes | Serves 4

- 1 ½ lbs.
- of salmon
- 4 teaspoons olive oil
- Pinch of sea salt

Dill Sauce:
- ½ cup non-fat Greek yogurt
- ½ cup light sour cream
- 2 tablespoons dill, finely chopped
- Pinch of sea salt

1. Preheat your air fryer to 270°Fahrenheit.
2. Cut salmon into four 6-ounce portions and drizzle 1 teaspoon of olive oil over each piece.
3. Season with sea salt.
4. Place salmon into cooking basket and cook for 23-minutes.
5. Make dill sauce.
6. In a mixing bowl, mix sour cream, yogurt, chopped dill and sea salt.
7. Top cooked salmon with sauce and garnish with additional dill and serve.

PER SERVING

Calories: 303 | Total Fat: 10.2g | Carbs: 8.9g | Protein: 14.8g

Allspices Salmon with Spices

Prep time: 10 minutes | Cook time: 15 minutes | Serves 4

- 1 teaspoon allspices
- 1-pound salmon
- 1 tablespoon avocado oil

1. Rub the salmon with allspices and sprinkle with avocado oil.
2. Put the salmon in the air fryer basket and cook at 360F for 15 minutes.

PER SERVING

Calories: 156 | Fat: 7.5 | Fiber: 0.3 | Carbs: 0.6 | Protein: 22.1

Spicy Fish Croquettes

Prep time: 15 minutes | Cook time:14 minutes |Serves 4

- 1 pound catfish, skinless, boneless and chopped
- 2 tablespoons olive oil
- 2 cloves garlic, minced
- 1 small onion, minced
- 1/4 cup all-purpose flour
- Sea salt and ground black pepper, to taste
- 1/2 cup breadcrumbs

1. Mix all ingredients in a bowl. Shape the mixture into bite-sized balls and place them in a lightly oiled Air Fryer cooking basket.
2. Cook the fish croquettes at 400 degrees F for about 14 minutes, shaking the basket halfway through the cooking time.
3. Bon appétit!

PER SERVING

Calories: 258 | Fat: 13.7g | Carbohydrates: 11.3g | Protein: 18.8g | Sugars: 1.6g | Fiber: 0.8g

Parmesan-Crusted Tilapia

Prep time: 5 minutes | Cook time: 5 minutes | Serves 4

- 1 tablespoon olive oil
- 4 tilapia fillets
- ¾ cup grated Parmesan cheese
- 1 tablespoon parsley, chopped
- 2 teaspoons paprika
- Pinch of garlic powder

1. Preheat your air fryer to 350°Fahrenheit.
2. Brush oil over tilapia fillets.
3. Mix the remaining ingredients in a bowl.
4. Coat tilapia fillets with parmesan mixture.
5. Line baking dish with parchment paper and arrange fillets.
6. Place in air fryer and cook for 5-minutes.

PER SERVING

Calories: 300 | Total Fat: 10.2g | Carbs: 9.8g | Protein: 15.6g

Salmon Croquettes

Prep time: 5 minutes | Cook time: 10 minutes | Serves 4

- 14-ounce tin of red salmon, drained
- 2 free-range eggs
- 5 tablespoons olive oil
- ½ cup breadcrumbs
- 2 tablespoons spring onions, chopped
- Salt and pepper to taste
- Pinch of herbs

7. Add drained salmon into a bowl and mash well.
8. Break in the egg, add herbs, spring onions, salt, pepper and mix well.
9. In another bowl, combine breadcrumbs and oil and mix well.
10. Take a spoon of the salmon mixture and shape it into a croquette shape in your hand.
11. Roll it in the breadcrumbs and place inside air fryer.
12. Set your air fryer to 390°Fahrenhiet for 10-minutes.

PER SERVING

Calories: 298 | Total Fat: 8.9g | Carbs: 7.6g | Protein: 15.2g

Southern-Style Shrimp

Prep time: 15 minutes | Cook time:10 minutes |Serves 4

- 1 cup all-purpose flour
- 1 teaspoon Old Bay seasoning
- Sea salt and lemon pepper, to taste
- 1/2 cup buttermilk
- 1 cup seasoned breadcrumbs
- 1 ½ pounds shrimp, peeled and deveined

1. In a shallow bowl, mix the flour, spices, and buttermilk. Place the seasoned breadcrumbs in the second bowl.
2. Dip the shrimp in the flour mixture, then in the breadcrumbs until they are well coated on all sides.
3. Arrange the shrimp in a well-greased Air Fryer cooking basket.
4. Cook the shrimp at 400 degrees F for about 10 minutes, shaking the basket halfway through the cooking time.
5. Bon appétit!

PER SERVING

Calories: 381| Fat: 1.4g | Carbohydrates: 45.2g | Protein: 39.8g | Sugars: 5.2g | Fiber: 5.4g

Cajun-Seasoned Lemon Salmon

Prep time: 5 minutes | Cook time: 7 minutes | Serves 1

- 1 salmon fillet
- 1 teaspoon Cajun seasoning
- 2 lemon wedges, for serving
- 1 teaspoon liquid stevia
- ½ lemon, juiced

1. Preheat your air fryer to 350°Fahrenheit.
2. Combine lemon juice and liquid stevia and coat salmon with this mixture.
3. Sprinkle Cajun seasoning all over salmon.
4. Place salmon on parchment paper in air fryer and cook for 7-minutes.
5. Serve with lemon wedges.

PER SERVING

Calories: 287 | Total Fat: 9.3g | Carbs: 8.4g | Protein: 15.3g

Trout with Mint

Prep time: 21 minutes | Cook time: 8 minutes | Serves 4

- 4 rainbow trout
- 1/3 pine nuts
- 3 garlic cloves; minced
- ½ cup mint; chopped.
- 1 cup olive oil+ 3 tbsp.
- 1 cup parsley; chopped
- Zest of 1 lemon
- Juice of 1 lemon
- A pinch of salt and pepper

6. Pat dry the trout, season with salt and pepper, and rub with 3 tbsp. of oil.
7. Put the fish in the Air Fryer's basket and cook for eight minutes on each side.
8. Divide the fish between plates and drizzle half of the lemon juice all over.
9. In a blender, combine the rest of the oil with the remaining lemon juice, parsley, garlic, mint, pine nuts, lemon zest, and pulse well. Spread this over the trout.

PER SERVING

CALORIES:240 | FAT: 12 G | CARBOHY-DRATES: 6 G | PROTEIN: 9 G

Cod Fish Teriyaki with Oysters, Mushrooms & Veggies

Prep time: 15 minutes | Cook time: 10 minutes | Serves 2

- 1 tablespoon olive oil
- 6 pieces mini king oyster
- mushrooms, thinly sliced
- 2 slices (1-inch) codfish
- 1 Napa cabbage leaf, sliced
- 1 clove garlic, chopped
- Salt to taste
- 1 green onion, minced
- Veggies, steamed of your choice

Teriyaki Sauce:
1 teaspoon liquid stevia
2 tablespoons mirin
2 tablespoons soy sauce

1. Prepare teriyaki sauce by mixing all the ingredients in a bowl then set aside.
2. Grease the air fryer basket with oil.
3. Place the mushrooms, garlic, Napa cabbage leaf, and salt inside.
4. Layer the fish on top.
5. Preheat your air fryer to 360°Fahrenheit for 3-minutes.
6. Place the basket in air fryer and cook for 5-minutes.
7. Stir.
8. Pour the teriyaki sauce over ingredients in the basket.
9. Cook for an additional 5-minutes.
10. Serve with your choice of steamed veggies.

PER SERVING

Calories: 297 | Total Fat: 10.6g | Carbs: 9.2g | Protein: 14.2g

Rosemary Sea Scallops

Prep time: 10 minutes | Cook time:7 minutes |Serves 4

- 1 ½ pounds sea scallops
- 4 tablespoons butter, melted
- 1 tablespoon garlic, minced
- Sea salt and ground black pepper, to season
- 2 rosemary sprigs, leaves picked and chopped
- 4 tablespoons dry white wine

1. Toss all ingredients in a lightly greased Air Fryer cooking basket.
2. Cook the scallops at 400 degrees F for 7 minutes, tossing the basket halfway through the cooking time.
3. Bon appétit!

PER SERVING

Calories: 318| Fat: 15.1g |Carbohydrates: 11.1g | Protein: 32.7g |Sugars: 0.6g | Fiber: 0.4g

Cheesy Breaded Salmon

Prep time: 5 minutes | Cook time: 20 minutes | Serves 4

- 2 cups breadcrumbs
- 4 salmon fillets
- 2 eggs, beaten
- 1 cup Swiss cheese, shredded

4. Preheat your air fryer to 390°Fahrenheit.
5. Dip each salmon filet into eggs.
6. Top with Swiss cheese.
7. Dip into breadcrumbs, coating entire fish.
8. Put into an oven-safe dish and cook for 20-minutes.

PER SERVING

Calories: 296 | Total Fat: 9.2g | Carbs: 8.7g | Protein: 15.2g

Chapter 8

Vegetables

Tomatoes Salad

Prep time: 10 minutes | Cook time: 20 minutes |
Serves 2

- 2 tomatoes halved
- Cook spray
- Salt and black pepper
- 1 tsp. parsley, chopped
- 1 tsp. basil, chopped
- 1 tsp. oregano, chopped
- 1 tsp. rosemary, chopped
- 1 cucumber, chopped
- 1 green onion, chopped

1. Spray tomato halves with cook oil. Season with salt and pepper.
2. Place them in your Air Fryer's basket. Cook for 20 minutes at 320 degrees F.
3. Transfer tomatoes to a bowl. Add parsley, basil, oregano, rosemary, cucumber and onion, and toss.

PER SERVING

Calories:55 | Protein: 2.59 g | Fat: 0.67 g | Carbohydrates: 11.62 g

Easy Greek Briami (Ratatouille)

Prep time: 15 minutes | Cook time: 40 minutes |
Serves 6

- 2 russet potatoes, cubed
- ½ cup Roma tomatoes, cubed
- 1 eggplant, cubed
- 1 zucchini, cubed
- 1 red onion, chopped
- 1 red bell pepper, chopped
- 2 garlic cloves, minced
- 1 teaspoon dried mint
- 1 teaspoon dried parsley
- 1 teaspoon dried oregano
- ½ teaspoon salt
- ½ teaspoon black pepper
- ¼ teaspoon red pepper flakes
- ⅓ cup olive oil
- 1 (8-ounce) can tomato paste
- ¼ cup vegetable broth
- ¼ cup water

1. Preheat the air fryer to 320°F.
2. In a large bowl, combine the potatoes, tomatoes, eggplant, zucchini, onion, bell pepper, garlic, mint, parsley, oregano, salt, black pepper, and red pepper flakes.
3. In a small bowl, mix together the olive oil, tomato paste, broth, and water.
4. Pour the oil-and-tomato-paste mixture over the vegetables and toss until everything is coated.
5. Pour the coated vegetables into the air fryer basket in an even layer and roast for 20 minutes. After 20 minutes, stir well and spread out again. Roast for an additional 10 minutes, then repeat the process and cook for another 10 minutes.

PER SERVING

Calories: 280 | Total Fat: 13g | Saturated Fat: 2g | Protein: 6g | Total Carbohydrates: 40g | Fiber: 7g | Sugar: 12g | Cholesterol: 0mg

Golden Parsnip Sticks

Prep time: 20 minutes | Cook time:15 minutes

|Serves 4

- 1 pound parsnip, trimmed and cut into sticks
- 2 tablespoons olive oil
- 1 teaspoon garlic, minced
- 1 teaspoon turmeric powder
- 1 tablespoon Dijon mustard
- Sea salt and ground black pepper, to taste

1. Toss the parsnip with the remaining ingredients | place them in the Air Fryer cooking basket.
2. Cook the parsnip sticks at 400 degrees F for about 15 minutes, shaking the basket occasionally to ensure even cooking.
3. Serve warm and enjoy!

PER SERVING

Calories: 169 | Fat: 4.1g | Carbohydrates: 26.8g | Protein: 8.2g | Sugars: 4.9g | Fiber: 8.2g

Fried Celery Sticks

Prep time: 15 minutes | Cook time:15 minutes

|Serves 4

- 4 stalks celery, cleaned and cut into matchsticks
- Sea salt and ground black pepper, to taste
- 1 cup bread crumbs
- 2 tablespoons avocado oil

1. Toss the celery with the remaining ingredients | place them in the Air Fryer cooking basket.
2. Cook the celery sticks at 400 degrees F for about 15 minutes, shaking the basket occasionally to ensure even cooking.
3. Serve warm and enjoy!

PER SERVING

Calories: 176 | Fat: 8.4g | Carbohydrates: 21.5g | Protein: 3.9g | Sugars: 2.6g | Fiber: 1.7g

Greek-Style Vegan Burgers

Prep time: 20 minutes | Cook time:15 minutes

|Serves 4

- 1 tablespoon ground chia seeds
- 14 ounces canned chickpeas, rinsed and drained
- 1/4 cup fresh coriander
- 1/4 cup fresh scallions
- 1 tablespoon rosemary
- 1 tablespoon thyme
- 1 tablespoon basil
- 2 garlic cloves, peeled
- 1/2 teaspoon ground cumin
- Sea salt and ground black pepper, to taste
- 2 tablespoons fresh lemon juice

1. To make a flax egg, soak the ground flaxseeds in 2 tablespoons of water for 15 minutes.
2. In your blender or food processor, mix all the ingredients, including the flax egg, until everything is well incorporated.
3. Form the mixture into patties and place them in a lightly greased Air Fryer cooking basket.
4. Air fry the patties at 380 degrees F for about 15 minutes, turning them over halfway through the cooking time.
5. Bon appétit!

PER SERVING

Calories: 169 | Fat: 4.1g | Carbohydrates: 26.8g |Protein: 8.2g | Sugars: 4.9g |Fiber: 8.2g

Greek Potato

Prep time: 10 minutes | Cook time: 20 minutes | Serves 4

- 1½ pounds potatoes, peeled and cubed
- Two tbsp. olive oil
- One tbsp. hot paprika
- 2 ounces coconut cream
- Salt and black pepper

1. Place potatoes in a bowl and add water to cover. Set them aside for 10 minutes.
2. Drain and mix with half of the oil, salt, pepper, and paprika and toss.
3. Place the potatoes in the basket of your Air Fryer. Cook at 360 degrees F for 20 minutes.
4. In a bowl, mix the coconut cream with salt, pepper and the rest of the oil and mix well.
5. Divide the potatoes among the plates. Add the coconut cream on top.

PER SERVING

Calories:203 | Protein: 4 g | Fat: 7.1 g | Carbohydrates: 32.2 g

Italian Herb Potatoes

Prep time: 25 minutes | Cook time:20 minutes |Serves 4

- 1 pound potatoes, peeled and cut into wedges
- 2 tablespoons olive oil
- 1 teaspoon granulated garlic
- 1 tablespoon Italian herb mix
- 1 teaspoon cayenne pepper
- Kosher salt and freshly ground black pepper, to taste

1. Toss the potatoes with the remaining ingredients until well coated on all sides. Arrange the potatoes in the Air Fryer basket.

2. Cook the potatoes at 400 degrees F for about 20 minutes, shaking the basket halfway through the cooking time.
3. Bon appétit!

PER SERVING

Calories: 149| Fat: 6.8g | Carbohydrates: 20.3g | Protein: 2.3g | Sugars: 0.9g | Fiber: 2.6g

Broccoli Vegan Tempura

Prep time: 10 minutes | Cook time:6 minutes |Serves 4

- 1 cup all-purpose flour
- 1/2 cup beer
- 2 tablespoons sesame oil
- 1/2 teaspoon cayenne pepper
- 1 teaspoon chili powder
- Sea salt and ground black pepper, to taste
- 1 pound broccoli florets

1. In a mixing bowl, thoroughly combine the flour, beer, oil, and spices.
2. Dip the broccoli florets in the tempura mixture and place them in a lightly oiled Air Fryer cooking basket.
3. Cook the broccoli florets at 395 degrees F for 6 minutes, shaking the basket halfway through the cooking time.
4. Bon appétit!

PER SERVING

Calories: 232 | Fat: 7.6g | Carbohydrates: 33.8g | Protein: 6.9g | Sugars: 2.6g | Fiber: 4.3g

Basic Fried Cucumber

Prep time: 20 minutes | Cook time:15 minutes
|Serves 4

- 2 cucumbers, sliced
- 2 tablespoons olive oil
- 1/2 cup cornmeal
- Sea salt and ground black pepper, to taste

1. Toss the cucumbers with the remaining ingredients | place them in the Air Fryer cooking basket.
2. Cook the cucumbers at 400 degrees F for about 15 minutes, shaking the basket occasionally to ensure even cooking.
3. Serve warm and enjoy!

PER SERVING

Calories: 144 |Fat: 7.2g | Carbohydrates: 17.5g | Protein: 1.9g | Sugars: 1.6g | Fiber: 1.5g

Fried Green Beans

Prep time: 10 minutes | Cook time:6 minutes
|Serves 3

- 3/4 pound green beans, trimmed and halved
- 1/2 cup vegan mayonnaise
- 1 teaspoon granulated garlic
- 1 teaspoon paprika
- Kosher salt and ground black pepper, to taste

1. Toss the green beans with the remaining ingredients until well coated on all sides.
2. Air fry the green beans at 390 degrees F for about 6 minutes, tossing the basket halfway through the cooking time.
3. Enjoy!

PER SERVING

Calories: 174 | Fat: 13.1g | Carbohydrates: 12.2g | Protein: 4.9g | Sugars: 4.8g | Fiber: 4g

Mediterranean Veggie Mix

Prep time: 10 minutes | Cook time: 20 minutes |
Serves 4

- 1 large zucchini, sliced
- 1 green pepper, sliced
- 1 large parsnip, peeled and cubed
- Salt and black pepper to taste
- 2 tablespoons honey
- 2 cloves garlic, crushed
- 1 teaspoon mixed herbs
- 1 teaspoon mustard
- 6 tablespoons olive oil, divided
- 4 cherry tomatoes
- 1 medium carrot, peeled and cubed

1. Add the zucchini, green pepper, parsnip, cherry tomatoes, carrot to bottom of air fryer.
2. Cover ingredients with 3 tablespoons of oil and adjust the time to 15-minutes.
3. Cook at 360°Fahrenheit.
4. Prepare your marinade by combining remaining ingredients in air fryer safe baking dish.
5. Combine marinade and vegetables in baking dish and stir well.
6. Sprinkle with salt and pepper.
7. Cook it at 390°Fahrenheit for 5-minutes.

PER SERVING

Calories: 262 | Total Fat: 11.3g | Carbs: 9.5g | Protein: 7.4g

Chapter 9

Snacks and Appetizers

Olive Oil Cake

Prep time: 5 minutes | Cook time: 15 minutes | Serves 4

- Olive oil cooking spray
- 1½ cups whole wheat flour, plus more for dusting
- 3 eggs
- ⅓ cup honey
- ½ cup olive oil
- ½ cup unsweetened almond milk
- ½ teaspoon vanilla extract
- ½ teaspoon almond extract
- 1 teaspoon baking powder
- ½ teaspoon salt

1. Preheat the air fryer to 380°F. Lightly coat the interior of an 8-by-8-inch baking dish with olive oil cooking spray and a dusting of whole wheat flour. Knock out any excess flour.
2. In a large bowl, beat the eggs and honey until smooth.
3. Slowly mix in the olive oil, then the almond milk, and finally the vanilla and almond extracts until combined.
4. In a separate bowl, whisk together the flour, baking powder, and salt.
5. Slowly incorporate the dry ingredients into the wet ingredients with a rubber spatula until combined, making sure to scrape down the sides of the bowl as you mix.
6. Pour the batter into the prepared pan and place it in the air fryer. Bake for 12 to 15 minutes, or until a toothpick inserted in the center comes out clean.

PER SERVING

Calories: 546 | Total Fat: 32g | Saturated Fat: 5g | Protein: 12g | Total Carbohydrates: 58g | Fiber: 4g | Sugar: 24g | Cholesterol: 140mg

Air Fryer Nuts

Prep time: 10 Minutes | Cook time: 4 minutes | Serves 2

- 2 cup mixed nuts
- 1 tablespoon olive oil
- 1/4 teaspoon cayenne
- 1 teaspoon ground cumin
- 1 teaspoon pepper
- 1 teaspoon salt

1. In a bowl, add all ingredients and stir well. Add the nuts mixture to the Air Fryer basket.
2. Place a baking pan on the oven rack. Set to air fry at 350 degrees F and cook for four minutes.

PER SERVING

CALORIES: 953 | FAT: 88.2 G | CARBOHYDRATES:33.3 G

Air Fried Olives

Prep time: 10 Minutes | Cook time: 5 minutes | Serves 4

- 2 cups olives
- 2 teaspoon garlic, minced
- 2 tablespoon olive oil
- 1/2 teaspoon dried oregano
- Salt and Pepper

1. Add olives and remaining ingredients into the bowl and stir well.
2. Add to the Air Fryer basket. Set to air fry at 300°F and cook for 5 minutes.

PER SERVING

CALORIES: 140 | FAT: 14.2 G | CARBOHYDRATES:4.8 G

Air-Fried Apricots In Whiskey Sauce

Prep time: 5 minutes | Cook time: 35 minutes | Serves 4

- 1 lb. apricot, pitted and halved
- ¼ cup whiskey
- 1 teaspoon pure vanilla extract
- ½ stick butter, room temperature
- ½ cup maple syrup sugar-free

1. In a small saucepan over medium heat, heat the maple syrup, vanilla, butter; simmer until the butter is melted.
2. Add the whiskey and stir to combine.
3. Arrange the apricots on the bottom of lightly greased baking dish.
4. Pour the sauce over the apricots; scatter whole cloves over the top.
5. Then, transfer the baking dish to the pre-heated air-fryer.
6. Air-fry at 380°Fahrenheit for 35-minutes.

PER SERVING

Calories: 356 | Total Fat: 17g | Carbs: 43.3g | Protein: 38.2g

Chickpea & Zucchini Burgers

Prep time: 15 minutes | Cook time: 10 minutes | Serves 4

- 1 can of chickpeas, strained
- 1 red onion, diced
- 2 eggs, beaten
- 1-ounce almond flour
- 3 tablespoons coriander
- 1 teaspoon garlic puree
- 1-ounce cheddar cheese, shredded
- 1 Courgette, spiralized
- 1 teaspoon chili powder
- Salt and pepper to taste
- 1 teaspoon mixed spice
1. Add your ingredients to a bowl and mix well.
2. Shape portions of the mixture into burgers.
3. Place in the air fryer for 15-minutes until cooked.

PER SERVING

Calories: 263 | Total Fat: 11.2g | Carbs: 8.3g | Protein: 6.3g

Sea Salt Beet Chips

Prep time: 10 minutes | Cook time: 30 minutes | Serves 6

- 4 medium beets, rinse and sliced thin
- 1 teaspoon sea salt
- 2 tablespoons olive oil
- Hummus, for serving

1. Preheat the air fryer to 380°F.
2. In a large bowl, toss the beets with sea salt and olive oil until well coated.
3. Put the beet slices into the air fryer and spread them out in a single layer.
4. Fry for 10 minutes. Stir, then fry for an additional 10 minutes. Stir again, then fry for a final 5 to 10 minutes, or until the chips reach the desired crispiness.
5. Serve with a favorite hummus.

PER SERVING

Calories: 63 | Total Fat: 5g | Saturated Fat: 1g | Protein: 1g | Total Carbohydrates: 5g | Fiber: 2g | Sugar: 3g | Cholesterol: 0mg

Date & Hazelnut Cookies

Prep time: 5 minutes | Cook time: 20 minutes | Serves 10

- 3 tablespoons sugar-free maple syrup
- 1/3 cup dated, dried
- ¼ cup hazelnuts, chopped
- 1 stick butter, room temperature
- ½ cup almond flour
- ½ cup corn flour
- 2 tablespoons Truvia for baking
- ½ teaspoon vanilla extract
- 1/3 teaspoon ground cinnamon
- ½ teaspoon cardamom

4. Firstly, cream the butter with Truvia and maple syrup until mixture is fluffy.
5. Sift both types of flour into bowl with butter mixture.
6. Add remaining ingredients.
7. Now, knead the mixture to form a dough; place in the fridge for 20-minutes.
8. To finish, shape the chilled dough into bite-size balls; arrange them on a baking dish and flatten balls with back of spoon.
9. Bake the cookies for 20-minutes at 310°Fahrenheit.

PER SERVING

Calories: 187 | Total Fat: 10.5g | Carbs: 23.2g | Protein: 1.5g

Coconut Strawberry Fritters

Prep time: 5 minutes | Cook time: 4 minutes | Serves 8

- ¾ cup almond flour
- ½ teaspoon baking powder
- ½ teaspoon coconut extract
- 1¼ cups soy milk
- 1/8 teaspoon salt
- 2 tablespoons Truvia for baking
- ¾ lb. strawberries

- 3 tablespoons coconut oil

1. Thoroughly combine all ingredients in a bowl.
2. Next, drop teaspoon amounts of the mix into air-fryer cooking basket; air-fry for 4-minutes at 345°Fahrenheit.

PER SERVING

Calories: 145 | Total Fat: 6g | Carbs: 20.7g | Protein: 2.8g

Parmesan Chicken Meatballs

Prep time: 5 minutes | Cook time: 10 minutes | Serves 4

- ½ cup whole-wheat breadcrumbs
- Pepper and salt to taste
- ½ lime, zested
- 1/3 cup parmesan cheese, grated
- ½ teaspoon paprika
- 1 teaspoon basil, dried
- 3 garlic cloves, minced
- ½ lb. ground chicken
- 1/3 teaspoon mustard seeds
- 1 ½ tablespoons melted butter
- 2 eggs, beaten

1. In a non-stick skillet that is preheated over medium heat, place ground chicken, garlic and cook until chicken is no longer pink, about 5-minutes.
2. Throw the remaining ingredients into skillet.
3. Remove from heat.
4. Allow to cool down and roll into balls.
5. Roll each ball into beaten eggs, then roll them in breadcrumbs and transfer them into the air-fryer basket.
6. Cook for 8-minutes at 385°Fahrenheit.

PER SERVING

Calories: 52 | Total Fat: 2.46g | Carbs: 2.94g | Protein: 7.8g

Glass Noodle & Tiger Shrimp Salad

Prep time: 15 minutes | Cook time: 8 minutes | Serves 4

- 12 tiger shrimps, butterflied
- Zest of one lemon
- Zest of one lime
- ¼ cup olive oil
- 2 tablespoons mixed spice
- 2 tablespoons olive oil
- A handful of basil, fried for garnish

For the salad:
- 4 baby yellow bell peppers, sliced
- 4 baby red bell peppers, sliced
- 2 scallions, bias cut
- 2 cups green papaya, peeled, seeded, julienned
- ½ cup mint leaves
- ½ cup cilantro leaves
- 16-ounces of glass noodles, cooked and chilled
- 1 English cucumber, peeled, seeded, sliced
- 1 carrot, peeled and julienned
- 2 tablespoons basil leaves, julienned

For dressing:
- 4-ounces of honey
- 2 cups grapeseed oil
- 1 cup soy sauce
- 4-ounces ginger, peeled and grated
- 1 bunch scallions, sliced
- 2 tablespoons of sweet chili sauce

1. Preheat your air-fryer to 390°Fahrenheit for 10-minutes.
2. Mix olive oil and mixed spice and brush mixture over shrimp.
3. Sprinkle the lemon and lime juice over the shrimps.
4. Season with salt and pepper.
5. Place the shrimp in the basket and cook for 4-minutes.
6. Chill shrimps on a plate and repeat cooking process with remaining shrimp.
7. Whisk lemon juice, soy sauce, honey, ginger, scallion and sweet chili sauce in a bowl.
8. Whisk in oil.
9. Add mixture to blend and mix to get a puree consistency.
10. Season to taste.
11. In a bowl, toss mixed greens and salad dressing mix, along with noodles, then divide it between serving plates.
12. Top each plate of salad with 3 shrimps.
13. Garnish with cilantro and basil.

PER SERVING

Calories: 258 | Total Fat: 15.89g | Carbs: 4.41g | Protein: 23.59g

Pecan Nutella

Prep time: 20 minutes | Cook time: 5 minutes |Serves 4

- 4 pecans, chopped
- 5 teaspoons butter, softened
- ½ teaspoon vanilla extract
- 1 tablespoon Splenda
- 1 teaspoon of cocoa powder

1. Put all ingredients in the air fryer and stir gently.
2. Cook the mixture at 400F for 5 minutes.
3. Then transfer the mixture in the serving bowl and refrigerate for 15-20 minutes before serving.

PER SERVING

Calories: 157 | Fat: 14.8 | Fiber: 1.6 | Carbs: 5.3 | Protein: 1.6

Delicious Clafoutis

Prep time: 15 minutes | Cook time: 25 minutes | Serves 6

- ¼ teaspoon nutmeg, grated
- ½ teaspoon crystalized ginger
- 1/3 teaspoon ground cinnamon
- ½ teaspoon baking soda
- ½ teaspoon baking powder
- 2 tablespoons Truvia for baking
- ½ cup coconut cream
- ¾ cup coconut milk
- 3 eggs, whisked
- 4 medium-sized pears, cored and sliced
- 1 ½ cups plums, pitted
- ¾ cup almond flour

1. Lightly grease 2 mini pie pans using a non-stick cooking spray.
2. Lay the plums and pears on the bottom of pie pans.
3. In a saucepan that is preheated over medium heat, warm the cream along with the coconut milk until thoroughly heated.
4. Remove the pan from heat; mix in the flour along with baking soda and baking powder.
5. In a bowl, mix the eggs, Truvia, spices until the mixture is creamy.
6. Add the creamy milk mixture.
7. Carefully spread this mixture over your fruit in pans.
8. Bake at 320°Fahrenheit for 25-minutes.

PER SERVING

Calories: 354 | Total Fat: 9.6g | Carbs: 66.6g | Protein: 6.2g

Broccoli with Cheese & Olives

Prep time: 5 minutes | Cook time: 15 minutes | Serves 4

- 2lbs. broccoli florets
- ¼ cup parmesan cheese, shaved
- 2 teaspoons lemon zest, grated
- 1/3 cup Kalamata olives, halved, pitted
- ½ teaspoon ground black pepper
- 1 teaspoon sea salt
- 2 tablespoons olive oil

1. Boil the water in a pan and cook the broccoli for 4-minutes.
2. Drain broccoli.
3. Toss the broccoli with oil, salt, and pepper.
4. Place broccoli in your air fryer basket and cook for 15-minutes at 400°Fahrenheit.
5. Toss twice during cook time.
6. Move to a serving bowl and toss in lemon zest, olives, and cheese.

PER SERVING

Calories: 242 | Total Fat: 7.2g | Carbs: 3.2g | Protein: 5.6g

Greece Style Cake

Prep time: 10 minutes | Cook time: 30 minutes |Serves 12

- 6 eggs, beaten
- 1 teaspoon vanilla extract
- 1 teaspoon baking powder
- 2 cups almond flour
- 4 tablespoons Erythritol
- 1 cup Plain yogurt

1. Mix all ingredients in the mixing bowl.
2. Then pour the mixture in the air fryer and flatten it gently.
3. Cook the cake at 350F for 30 minutes.

PER SERVING

Calories: 159 | Fat: 11.3 | Fiber: 2 | Carbs: 5.9 | Protein: 7.9

Air-Fried Fingerling Potatoes

Prep time: 5 minutes | Cook time: 30 minutes | Serves 4

- 2 lbs. Fingerling potatoes, peeled, cubed
- 2 tablespoons chives, minced
- 2 tablespoons parsley leaves, minced
- 2 garlic cloves, smashed
- 2 tablespoons butter, melted
- 1 shallot, quartered

1. Add cubed potatoes to an oven-proof dish.
2. Brush potatoes with melted butter.
3. Sprinkle with cubed potatoes the rest of ingredients.
4. Set your air-fryer for 320°Fahrenheit and cook for 30-minutes.
5. Stir a few times during cook time.
6. Serve warm.

PER SERVING

Calories: 213 | Total Fat: 5.2g | Carbs: 32.1g | Protein: 4.68g

Coconut Prune Cookies

Prep time: 10 minutes | Cook time: 20 minutes | Serves 10

- ½ teaspoon baking soda
- ½ teaspoon baking powder
- ½ teaspoon orange zest
- 1 teaspoon vanilla paste
- 1/3 teaspoon ground cinnamon
- 1 stick butter, softened
- 1 ½ cups almond flour
- 2 tablespoons Truvia for baking
- 1/3 cup prunes, chopped
- 1/3 coconut, shredded

1. Mix the butter with Truvia until mixture becomes fluffy; sift in the flour and add baking powder, as well as baking soda.

2. Add the remaining ingredients and combine well.
3. Knead the dough and transfer it to the fridge for 20-minutes.
4. To finish, shape the chilled dough into bite-size balls; arrange the balls on a baking dish and gently flatten them with the back of a spoon.
5. Air-fry for 20-minutes at 315°Fahrenheit.

PER SERVING

Calories: 227 | Total Fat: 10.3g | Carbs: 32.5g | Protein: 2.3g

Chocolate Cream

Prep time: 10 minutes | Cook time: 15 minutes | Serves 3

- 1 oz dark chocolate, chopped
- 1 cup coconut cream
- 1 teaspoon vanilla extract
- 1 tablespoon Erythritol

1. Pour coconut cream in the air fryer.
2. Add chocolate, vanilla extract, and Erythritol.
3. Cook the chocolate cream for 15 minutes at 360F. Stir the liquid from time to time during cooking.

PER SERVING

Calories: 236 | Fat: 21.9 | Fiber: 2 | Carbs: 10.3 | Protein: 2.6

Spicy Cheesy Breaded Mushrooms

Prep time: 5 minutes | Cook time: 7 minutes | Serves 22

- 8-ounces of Button mushrooms (pat dried)
- 1 egg
- Almond flour as required
- 3-ounces parmesan cheese, freshly grated
- Breadcrumbs as needed
- Salt and pepper to taste
- 1 teaspoon paprika

1. Mix the cheese and the breadcrumbs and paprika in a mixing bowl.
2. Whisk the egg in another bowl.
3. Dredge the Button mushrooms in the flour, dip in egg then coat them in breadcrumb mix.
4. Cook for 7-minutes in your air fryer at 360° Fahrenheit, tossing once halfway through cook time.

PER SERVING

Calories: 203 | Total Fat: 4.2g | Carbs: 3.2g | Protein: 3.6g

Air-Fried Ratatouille

Prep time: 5 minutes | Cook time: 15 minutes | Serves 4

- 1 onion, peeled, cubed
- 1 clove garlic, crushed
- 1 tablespoon olive oil
- 2 tomatoes, chopped
- Fresh ground pepper
- 2 teaspoons Provencal herbs
- 1 large zucchini, sliced
- 1 yellow bell pepper, chopped

1. Preheat your air-fryer to 300°Fahrenheit.
2. In an oven-proof bowl, add vegetables, salt, pepper and olive oil and mix well.
3. Put the bowl in the basket in air fryer.

4. Cook for 15-minutes, stirring halfway through cook time.
5. Serve with fricasseed meat.

PER SERVING

Calories: 154 | Total Fat: 12.05g | Carbs: 11.94g | Protein: 1.69g

Spanish Style Spiced Potatoes

Prep time: 15 minutes | Cook time: 23 minutes | Serves 4

- 3 potatoes, peeled and chopped into chips
- 1 onion, diced
- ½ cup tomato sauce
- 1 tomato, thinly sliced
- 1 tablespoon red wine vinegar
- 2 tablespoons olive oil
- 1 teaspoon paprika
- 1 teaspoon chili powder
- Salt and pepper to taste
- 1 teaspoon rosemary
- 1 teaspoon oregano
- 1 teaspoon mixed spice
- 2 teaspoons coriander

1. Toss the chips in the olive oil and cook in your air fryer for 15-minutes at 360°Fahrenheit.
2. Mix remaining ingredients in a baking dish.
3. Place the sauce in air fryer for 8-minutes.
4. Toss the potatoes in the sauce and serve warm!

PER SERVING

Calories: 265 | Total Fat: 7,3g | Carbs: 6.2g | Protein: 5.2g

Appendix 1 Measurement Conversion Chart

Volume Equivalents (Dry)	
US STANDARD	**METRIC (APPROXIMATE)**
1/8 teaspoon	0.5 mL
1/4 teaspoon	1 mL
1/2 teaspoon	2 mL
3/4 teaspoon	4 mL
1 teaspoon	5 mL
1 tablespoon	15 mL
1/4 cup	59 mL
1/2 cup	118 mL
3/4 cup	177 mL
1 cup	235 mL
2 cups	475 mL
3 cups	700 mL
4 cups	1 L

Volume Equivalents (Liquid)		
US STANDARD	**US STANDARD (OUNCES)**	**METRIC (AP-PROXIMATE)**
2 tablespoons	1 fl.oz.	30 mL
1/4 cup	2 fl.oz.	60 mL
1/2 cup	4 fl.oz.	120 mL
1 cup	8 fl.oz.	240 mL
1 1/2 cup	12 fl.oz.	355 mL
2 cups or 1 pint	16 fl.oz.	475 mL
4 cups or 1 quart	32 fl.oz.	1 L
1 gallon	128 fl.oz.	4 L

Temperatures Equivalents	
FAHRENHEIT(F)	**CELSIUS(C) APPROXIMATE**
225 °F	107 °C
250 °F	120 ° °C
275 °F	135 °C
300 °F	150 °C
325 °F	160 °C
350 °F	180 °C
375 °F	190 °C
400 °F	205 °C
425 °F	220 °C
450 °F	235 °C
475 °F	245 °C
500 °F	260 °C

Weight Equivalents	
US STANDARD	**METRIC (APPROXIMATE)**
1 ounce	28 g
2 ounces	57 g
5 ounces	142 g
10 ounces	284 g
15 ounces	425 g
16 ounces (1 pound)	455 g
1.5 pounds	680 g
2 pounds	907 g

Appendix 2 The Dirty Dozen and Clean Fifteen

The Environmental Working Group (EWG) is a nonprofit, nonpartisan organization dedicated to protecting human health and the environment Its mission is to empower people to live healthier lives in a healthier environment. This organization publishes an annual list of the twelve kinds of produce, in sequence, that have the highest amount of pesticide residue-the Dirty Dozen-as well as a list of the fifteen kinds ofproduce that have the least amount of pesticide residue-the Clean Fifteen.

THE DIRTY DOZEN

The 2016 Dirty Dozen includes the following produce. These are considered among the year's most important produce to buy organic:

Strawberries	Spinach
Apples	Tomatoes
Nectarines	Bell peppers
Peaches	Cherry tomatoes
Celery	Cucumbers
Grapes	Kale/collard greens
Cherries	Hot peppers

The Dirty Dozen list contains two additional itemskale/collard greens and hot peppers-because they tend to contain trace levels of highly hazardous pesticides.

THE CLEAN FIFTEEN

The least critical to buy organically are the Clean Fifteen list. The following are on the 2016 list:

Avocados	Papayas
Corn	Kiw
Pineapples	Eggplant
Cabbage	Honeydew
Sweet peas	Grapefruit
Onions	Cantaloupe
Asparagus	Cauliflower
Mangos	

Some of the sweet corn sold in the United States are made from genetically engineered (GE) seedstock. Buy organic varieties of these crops to avoid GE produce.

Appendix 3 Index

Tracy G. Woolard

Printed in Great Britain
by Amazon

30249933R00044